CLEAN PLATES

New York City 2016

A Guide to the
Healthiest, Tastiest
and Most Sustainable
Restaurants for Vegetarians
and Carnivores

By JARED KOCH

WITH CONTRIBUTIONS BY LAUREN COULL

DISCLAIMER: I am not a medical doctor, and nothing in this book is intended to diagnose, treat or cure any medical condition, illness or disease. Anyone with a specific medical condition should consult a physician.

Published by Clean Plates
Palisades Park, NJ

Interior design by Gary Robbins

Printed in Canada

10 9 8 7 6 5 4 3 2 1

*Library of Congress
Cataloging-in-Publication Data:*

Koch, Jared.
  Clean Plates New York City 2016: A Guide to the Healthiest, Tastiest and Most Sustainable Restaurants for Vegetarians and Carnivores / by Jared Koch. – Palisades Park, NJ : Clean Plates, 2014.
  p.   cm.
  ISBN 978-0-9859221-8-4
  1. Food—Popular works.
  2. Diet—Popular works.
  3. Nutrition—Popular works.
  4. Restaurants—New York (State) —New York.
  I. Title.
TX355.K63   2014
641—dc22
2008940260

MIX
Paper from
responsible sources
FSC® C103567
www.fsc.org

CONTENTS

WHAT IS CLEAN PLATES?

A NOTE FROM JARED

WELCOME TO *CLEAN PLATES NYC 2016!*

I am excited to introduce you to *Clean Plates NYC*. For those already familiar with us, I'm thrilled to welcome you back. This guide includes the top 100 healthiest, tastiest and most sustainable restaurants in New York City.

Let's face it: We dine out a lot, and restaurants can be bad-eating minefields. But eating high-quality food that tastes delicious should not have to be challenging. No one actually wants to consume hormones, antibiotics or pesticides; it's just that searching for the good stuff takes time. That's where *Clean Plates NYC* comes in. We've done all the dirty work for you to make clean eating an easy, pleasurable and sacrifice-free adventure.

The good news is that restaurant trends are heading in the right direction, and there are more options than ever for clean eaters to choose from. We've seen an explosion of healthy fast-casual spots (great for grabbing a quick meal) and more neighborhood haunts and fine-dining establishments offering vegetable-centric menus. The long-disrespected "vegetarian option" has finally been invited to the table—and with it, more sustainably raised protein as well. Consumers (that's me and you) are getting smarter about what actually is healthy (lots more fresh-pressed juice and smoothie options) as opposed to what just sounds healthy (think fro-yo). And, most importantly to us here at Clean Plates, New York chefs' sourcing practices continue to improve as they deepen their understanding and commitment to how produce is grown and animals are raised.

Clean Plates NYC is about helping you make better, more informed choices. There's a lot of nutritional information out there, but it can be totally confusing. That's why this guide also provides an easy-to-follow overview of how to best eat clean while dining out.

5

A little about me: After deferring my acceptance to medical school and embarking on a decade-long stint as a successful entrepreneur, I decided that I needed to focus on my health and happiness. As part of that journey, I not only became a certified nutritional consultant but also healed myself from chronic irritable bowel syndrome (IBS), fatigue and skin issues. I've also had some amazing teachers: Andrew Weil, M.D.; Deepak Chopra; Dr. Mark Hyman; and Walter Willett, the Chair of the Department of Nutrition at Harvard; in addition to many experts in the fields of raw foods, Chinese medicine, Ayurveda, macrobiotics, vegetarianism and high-protein diets.

Thanks to my experiences, I've had several insights over the years about how we eat, which is the foundation on which Clean Plates has been built. I will share these insights with you throughout this guide.

I wrote this book because there's a real lack of helpful, well-organized information for people who want to dine more mindfully and still enjoy the experience of eating. Yes, cooking at home is important, and many nutrition books (including *The Clean Plates Cookbook*, as well as our website, CleanPlates.com) offer delicious recipes, but the truth is that we eat out a lot—it's just part of New York life. We created *Clean Plates NYC* to be the most well-researched, comprehensive and easy-to-use healthy dining guide that exists. I am certain it will help you navigate the ever-expanding maze of the city's healthiest, tastiest and most-sustainable restaurants.

Together, let's shatter the myth that healthier eating is a sacrifice and prove that we can do it without the guilt, inconvenience, boredom and sheer lack of long-term success that characterize the usual diets. You see, eating clean food is admirable, but I am equally interested in clean plates—that is, the kind of food that makes you want to lick the plate clean.

In good health,

CLEAN PLATES' MISSION is to make it easy and enjoyable for you to eat better. The first step is simply reminding yourself why you want to focus on your eating habits in the first place. There are a multitude of reasons why you may decide to eat better; at the end of the day it all comes down to choices. Here are some reasons to help you choose wisely and intentionally.

FOR PHYSICAL HEALTH AND QUALITY OF LIFE

Our health may be affected more by the foods we eat than by any other factor. This is great news, since it means we can do something about it. Of course, exercise, sleep and genetics—not to mention our relationships, career and spirituality—count, too. But the reason "you are what you eat" has endured as a phrase is because what we consume builds, fuels, cleanses or—unfortunately—pollutes our very cells.

If you're healthy, you're more likely to:

- have more energy to enjoy life and live to your fullest potential;
- enjoy greater mental clarity for work and play;
- maintain emotional equilibrium and a pleasant mood;
- suffer from fewer minor ailments such as colds and allergies;
- reduce your risk of contracting potentially fatal diseases like cancer, diabetes and heart disease;
- age more slowly and gracefully, staving off problems like arthritis and Alzheimer's disease;
- save money by having fewer healthcare bills and less time off work;
- have clearer skin and a trimmer physique (a little vanity never hurt anyone).

FOR THE WORLD BEYOND YOUR PLATE

Here's a new one: An organic apple a day keeps the greenhouse gases away. Translation? Eating clean is good for nature. When you start choosing cleaner foods, you can positively affect the planet. When you choose grass-fed meats, you are supporting farmers who employ humane practices. When you choose non-GMO certified products you are taking a stand against the enormous amount of pesticides it takes to grow GMO crops and the adverse effects of cross-contamination on both the land and wildlife.

And the icing on the cake (naturally sweetened, of course)? When we choose eco-friendly practices, most of the time it is also healthier for us.

CLEAN PLATES: MORE THAN JUST THIS GUIDE

SIGN UP FOR OUR EMAIL

Visit cleanplates.com and sign up to receive nutritional tips, recipes and behind-the-scene looks at your favorite Clean Plates establishments and chefs on both a national level and in NYC!

VISIT CLEANPLATES.COM

While this guide features the Clean Plates 100 NYC restaurants, our website showcases more than 2,000 establishments that emphasize clean eating and sustainability. Explore cleanplates.com for national content or browse by city (NYC and LA) for hundreds of restaurant reviews plus articles packed with food scene news, chef interviews, healthy eating tips, product picks, recipes and more.

DOWNLOAD OUR IPHONE APP

Our iPhone app with geolocation makes clean eating choices on the go—from fine dining to quick farm-to-fork eats—easier than ever. Choose from hundreds of restaurants based on location, cuisine or dietary needs.

BUY OUR COOKBOOK

Available at Amazon.com, Barnes and Noble and local retailers, *The Clean Plates Cookbook* offers sensible, sustainable and healthful home cooking tips and recipes for anyone interested in maintaining a clean lifestyle while dining in.

JUST AS THERE'S no one-size-fits-all diet for everyone, there's no one right way to read and use this book. But here are several helpful features.

TAKE IT WITH YOU EVERYWHERE

Constructed to be small and lightweight, *Clean Plates NYC* is easy to slip in a bag or back pocket, and its rounded corners will keep it from getting dog-eared. No matter where you are in NYC, you'll be able to quickly locate a restaurant that serves a healthy, delicious version of the cuisine you're in the mood for—from fast food to fine dining, vegan to BBQ and any combination thereof. Don't want to keep it on you? Store one at home and one at the office. (Hey, we won't stop you from buying two.)

LEARN MORE ABOUT CLEAN EATING

Check out the "Clean Plates Philosophy" section, preceding the restaurant reviews, where we outline the Five Keys to Clean Eating. This section provides an easy-to-follow education on how to best eat clean while dining out so you have a foundation from which you can make intelligent and informed choices to implement healthier eating habits immediately.

FIND YOUR PERFECT MATCH

We don't want anyone to be left out. So whether you're a vegetarian or meat-eater, want to eat gluten-free or not—and whether you want to spend lavishly or lightly—we've tracked down restaurants for you (always serving delicious meals, naturally). *Clean Plates NYC* boasts an incredibly diverse array of establishments (including full reviews) representing many different cuisines, budgets and geographic locations. There are many ways to find your perfect match:

BY ICON We have created special icons to indicate the restaurant's price point, whether it offers grab-and-go options, and/or delivery and whether the establishment offers gluten-free, vegetarian/vegan choices and/or specializes in thoughtfully procured animal proteins. See p. 65 for our icon key. You can search this book by icon using the index beginning on p. 179.

ALPHABETICALLY Restaurant reviews are presented alphabetically in this guide.

THE INDEX The index lets you quickly find what you are looking for in a variety of configurations—search by icons, geography, and even specific social situations like Brunch and Business Lunch. See p. 179.

TOP FIVES This year we've included the Top Fives page (p. 66) to help you easily find our favorite picks for specific dietary wants and needs like vegetarian/vegan and Paleo-friendly.

BEYOND RESTAURANTS Check out our favorite places to grab some organic pastries, fair-trade coffee, clean food-truck fare, ice cream, cold-pressed juice and artisanal provisions (p. 167).

DISCOVER HOW EATING WELL CAN BE FUN, STRESS-FREE AND LIFE-CHANGING

Use this guide to help you effortlessly eat healthier—since Clean Plates does the work for you—and put to rest the excuse that healthy foods are too inaccessible and expensive to incorporate into your life. When you start eating better food, you'll begin craving it and your body will respond by rewarding you with better moods, energy and health.

HOW WE CHOOSE THE RESTAURANTS

OVER THE YEARS NYC has become rich with options for clean dining. To accommodate this growth, as well as the demands of our readers, we decided to open up the selection process and not limit our picks to just one borough. What you have in your hands is a one-of-a-kind guide to the 100 best restaurants in NYC serving healthier dishes that pleased our food critics' discerning palates.

Our goal was to compile a wide-ranging list of healthy and sustainable NYC restaurants that accommodated both vegetarians and carnivores to meet your needs under many circumstances. We scoured other guidebooks, newsletters and websites, petitioned chefs and restaurateurs, and literally walked all over the city looking for discerning candidates. This produced a list of 500 restaurants! From there we subjected each restaurant on our master list to a health-screening process. Posing as a potential customer over the phone, we queried the staff about their preparation and sourcing methods. (Is your meat hormone- and antibiotic-free? Is it grass-fed? What is your apple pie sweetened with?) In addition, we thoroughly reviewed the menu online and in person.

If the restaurant passed this initial health test, we sent a survey to the chef, general manager or restaurant owner to gather even more specific information about ingredients and sourcing practices. Metrics were created to evaluate their responses, and our amazing food critics and writers—Tressa Eaton, Lauren Coull, Megan Murphy, Ashley Spivak, Marisa Robertson-Textor and Erin Hartigan—were sent to assess the highest-scoring establishments incognito to avoid special treatment.

A wide variety of food was ordered—appetizers, side dishes, main courses and desserts. In addition, the staff was asked more questions, both to fact-check our initial queries and to gather more information. Then, we sat down and assessed the restaurant from an editorial perspective (see what we took into consideration below). Again, our goal was to not only provide you with the healthiest, tastiest and most sustainable restaurants, but to also provide as much variety as possible. True, we may have missed a few—this is NYC after all, home to a dizzying array of eateries—but we tried to make it as comprehensive as possible.

Please note, we are not operating as a certifying agency. We have curated this guide to bring you an assortment of options based upon what we think will be most useful for a typical NYC lifestyle.

When choosing a restaurant, we took the following into account:

TASTE Part of the Clean Plates mission is to prove that healthy eating doesn't mean sacrificing taste. Therefore, we sent experienced food critics to each restaurant to ensure your taste buds will be as satisfied as your body.

ATMOSPHERE Whether you need a quick fix in the middle of the workday, are trying to impress a date or are looking to be pampered, we were sure to include a variety of establishments to meet all needs.

GEOGRAPHY Wherever you live, work, shop and hang out, we've identified a restaurant nearby that serves healthy and delicious meals. We tried to offer suggestions in as many parts of the city as we could.

CUISINE From Italian to Indian, French to gastropub, we tried our best to have you covered.

PRICE It was important to us to include restaurants in all price ranges, from less than $15 for a full meal to more than $60.

INGREDIENT SOURCING AND SUSTAINABILITY PRACTICES We look for restaurants that are transparent with their sourcing practices for animal products and produce, buy locally when possible, have a focus on organic ingredients, use high-quality cooking oils, salts and sweeteners, and don't have a large percentage of deep-fried foods on the menu. We also look for establishments that compost, filter their water, recycle, and are part of third-party associations such as City Harvest, the Green Restaurant Association and the Slow Food movement.

MENU OFFERINGS We believe that meals are meant to bring people together. Therefore we emphasize restaurants that offer vegetable-based *and* meat-centric dishes so that those with different dietary preferences can still dine together. We also look for establishments that cater to specific dietary needs like gluten-free and vegan.

If you stick to eating at these restaurants when you dine out, there's a good chance you'll improve your quality of life and your health. Why? For one thing, you'll be putting better foods into your body, and it will respond in kind. For another, you'll start to associate delicious meals with healthy meals— and you'll begin to crave the latter. Consuming junk food will seem less and less appealing. And you'll be doing all of this with little effort because the restaurants—and this guide—will have done the work for you. All you have to do is eat!

THE CLEAN PLATES PHILOSOPHY:
THE FIVE KEYS TO CLEAN EATING

We believe there is a dream diet for everyone—but it's not the same for each person. As nutrition pioneer Roger Williams wrote in his groundbreaking 1950s book *Biochemical Individuality*, "If we continue to try to solve problems on the basis of the average man, we will be continually in a muddle. Such a man does not exist."

We're all biochemically—genetically, hormonally and so on— different, and the idea that this should guide our eating habits has recently begun to excite the leading-edge medical and nutrition community. Experts are beginning to talk about the benefits of individualizing our diets rather than giving advice based on recommended daily allowances (RDA) or the U.S. Department of Agriculture's "My Plate," both created with the "average" person in mind.

EATING AS A BIO-INDIVIDUAL

The philosophy that no single way of eating is right for everyone isn't new. Both traditional Chinese medicine and India's Ayurvedic system revolve around prescribing the most appropriate diet for specific categories of body types and constitutions.

More recent incarnations of these ancient approaches include the blood-type diet and metabolic typing. The blood-type diet was made famous more than a decade ago by naturopath Peter D'Adamo, who theorized (to put it very simply) that people with type O blood do best eating meat, while those with type A thrive as vegetarians. The thinking behind the discovery? Those with type O descended from ancient hunters while those with type A came from agricultural civilizations. The idea behind metabolic typing (again, to put it simply) is that your metabolism dictates the appropriate percentage of proteins and carbohydrates in your diet. Those who metabolize proteins well require extra animal foods, while others do better with more carbs.

Not everyone takes the bio-individual approach. For example, proponents of *The China Study*, a 2005 book by two nutritional biochemists who conducted a 20-year survey of Chinese diets, argue that animal consumption is the leading cause of human disease and everyone would be better off if they cut back, while followers of Weston A. Price, a dentist who carried out extensive health research in many countries, rely on culturally based studies to back up their claim that animal proteins and organ meats have benefits. They suggest everyone would be better off incorporating more animal foods into their diet.

As you read through the list below of how we're all unique, some of the points may seem obvious. (Of course someone training for a marathon requires different foods than someone sitting in front of a computer all day, for instance.) But these distinctions manifest not only between individuals, but also between your different selves—your tired self, your active self and the like. Eating as a bio-individual means paying attention to how your body reacts to various foods and assessing for yourself how your unique body best thrives.

HOW WE DIFFER

GENETIC MAKEUP To a large extent, the anatomy and body chemistry you inherited from your ancestors determines your nutritional needs and ability to benefit from particular foods. For example, a few recent studies have shown that some people possess the genetic ability to metabolize caffeine more efficiently than others. Research has also revealed that specific groups of people have the genetic makeup to absorb vitamin B12 with ease, or benefit greatly from broccoli's cancer-fighting nutrients, while others lack that ability.

CULTURE AND BACKGROUND Your ethnicity and upbringing can influence how your body acts. For instance, many people whose families come from Asia are lactose intolerant. It's helpful to consider which foods are part of your culture and background and incorporate the appropriate ones into your diet.

LIFESTYLE You require different foods when training for a marathon than when you practice an hour of yoga each week.

DAY-TO-DAY PHYSICAL HEALTH Pay attention to your physical health symptoms to figure out what foods you need. Sick? Miso soup may be just the thing. Sneezing constantly? Avoid dairy and sugar; the former causes the body to produce mucus and the latter weakens the immune system.

GENDER Your gender affects your diet needs. For example, menstruating women require more iron than men, but men need more zinc than women to nourish their reproductive systems.

AGE A growing, active teen will be ravenous at dinnertime. The same person, 60 years later, will likely find that his appetite is waning.

SEASONS AND CLIMATE Even the weather affects what's best for you to eat. When it's hot outside, the body will likely crave cooling foods like salads; on a cold winter day, hot soup is more appealing.

HOW WE'RE THE SAME

Our food choices often become another way of separating us. When there are moral underpinnings to our choices, it's especially tempting to think "My way is the only right way to eat." While bio-individuality may seemingly highlight how we are different, these distinctions are only made to reach a shared goal—to thrive physically. Once this has been achieved, we've created an unshakable foundation for living to our fullest potential and for making a meaningful contribution to our collective well-being as a species and a planet.

Being different should bring us together. Why? Partially because it's about realizing that other people have needs distinct from ours. Some types love to begin their day with a shot of wheatgrass— but perhaps the thought makes you turn green. While your friends can't imagine living without an occasional hamburger or slice of pizza, you might thrive on hearty salads and raw foods. And we all know that irritating person who can gobble up everything in sight and remain slim—a profile that many of us don't have. Hopefully being aware of these distinctions will lead us to be less critical of others— and less likely to feel guilty about our own choices. Judgment and guilt, after all, are bad for your health. At the very least, they really mess with your digestion.

HOW SHOULD YOU APPROACH OTHER DIETARY THEORIES?

One diet (it's a stretch to call it a dietary theory!) that most of us would like to move away from is the standard American diet (aka SAD). So what should we move toward? We all have different needs, but that doesn't mean we have to invent diets from scratch. We have help: other established dietary theories.

Think of it as designing your own diet using bits and pieces of good, but different ideas, gathered from a variety of established theories. The point is that you don't need to adhere to any particular theory; each has its pros and cons, and none is right for everyone. Instead, tailor what you eat to your biology, body, hormones, tastes and way of looking at the world. The Five Keys to Clean Eating will help to guide your choices.

Bio-individuality means there is no perfect diet for everyone. There is, however, the perfect food for everyone—real food. It's what we're designed to eat, regardless of our lifestyle, genetic makeup and other differences. Which leads to the next Key to Clean Eating.

#2

The overwhelming majority of your diet should consist of natural, high-quality and whole foods.

WHICH MEANS … WHAT? What, exactly, is real food? Once upon a time it had an obvious answer, but, over the past hundred years, food has become increasingly unlike itself: processed, altered with chemicals, dyed unnatural colors, flavored with suspect ingredients and turned as artificial as can be. These kinds of changes generally result in more toxins and fewer nutrients. The success of diets like Paleo, macrobiotics and raw foods in claiming to help heal diabetes and even cancer (according to some studies) is due in large part to the fact that these diets call for increasing your intake of real, high quality, whole foods while reducing consumption of artificial and chemical-laden dishes.

TIP: DON'T GET SIDETRACKED BY FOCUSING ONLY ON CALORIES

Many people equate reducing calories with a healthier lifestyle, but Clean Plates firmly believes that the quality of the foods we eat are much more important—even when it comes to losing weight. Here's a way of looking at it: Think of food as fuel. Does a car run best on poor-quality fuel? Of course not. Our bodies are the same: They need optimal fuel. Another way of looking at it is to ask yourself: What's better for my body—a 150-calorie candy bar or 200 calories of vegetables?

All this means we desperately need to get back to the basics. So, what exactly is real food?

REAL/NATURAL FOODS

In this guide the terms 'real' and 'natural' are used synonymously to denote foods that are neither highly processed nor artificial. Knowing what's natural is largely a matter of intuition and common sense; it's not as if you're going to start bringing a checklist to restaurants.

Nevertheless, you'll become a pro at identifying the real thing more quickly if you ask yourself a couple of questions the next time you eat: What would I eat if I lived in the wild? What has the earth and nature provided for humans to eat? What have I, as a human, evolved to eat? To keep it simple, focus on what grows out of the ground or on a tree. In addition, think vegetables, fruits, nuts, seeds, beans, grains, herbs and animal foods.

TIP: AN EASY WAY TO FIGURE OUT IF IT'S REAL FOOD

Ask yourself this question: Was it made in nature or in a factory? Visualize where the item began its life. Perhaps you'll see it hanging on a bush, growing on a tree, sprouting up from the earth or grazing in a field. If it's fizzing to life in a test tube, move on.

NOT ALL REAL/NATURAL FOODS ARE EQUAL

While the goal is to incorporate as many real foods into the diet as possible, there are a few things to think about to ensure you are getting the most out of your food.

IS IT A WHOLE FOOD?

Generally speaking, the less heat, pressure and processing a food is exposed to, the more whole it is. But this doesn't necessarily mean we should only consume raw foods. For some foods the nutrients are most bioavailable in their raw state; for others, some exposure to low heat actually breaks down the food's cell walls and fiber, making it easier for our bodies to absorb the nutrients.

Because there are benefits to consuming both cooked and raw foods, we should aim to incorporate both into our diets. The ratio will ultimately depend on the strength of your digestive system and personal tastes.

When examining the wholeness of a prepared dish, you should consider:

- The cooking methods used. Err on the side of undercooking, since prolonged exposure to high heat destroys nutrients, enzymes and water content. Examples: Steaming or poaching (good) versus boiling (not good) or deep frying (bad).
- The ingredients. Examples: A bowl of berries (good) versus fruit juice with sugar (not good).
- The number of steps or processes used to make the food. Examples: A bowl of oatmeal made from steel-cut oats (good) versus cereal made into flakes (not so good).

IS IT A HIGH QUALITY FOOD?

A peach from the grocery store is a real-food item—it was made in nature and wasn't flavored in a factory—but that doesn't mean it's the best quality. There's a difference if that peach was irradiated and artificially ripened or if that peach was grown organically and locally. In the former, you'd be ingesting produce with an altered chemical structure, fewer nutrients and more pesticides, whereas in the latter you'd be ingesting chemical-free, highly nutritious, fresh fruit.

In addition, ask yourself if additives, flavorings, coloring or preservatives were used. It's not always obvious in a restaurant, but it's worth considering. For instance, are those fresh peaches in your pie, or are they from a can?

WHAT'S MORE IMPORTANT: LOCALLY GROWN OR ORGANIC?

Organic but non-local produce is free of pesticides harmful to our bodies and the soil, but it requires extra energy to travel from farm-to-table and loses nutrients along the way. Locally grown but non-organic goods retain most of their nutrients because of the speed at which they get to our plates, but they may be sprayed with chemicals that are damaging to our bodies, the soil and the atmosphere.

If you can't get an item locally grown *and* organic, there is no easy answer. It is a matter of personal choice, and if you choose one or the other you are doing pretty good.

TIP: A WORD OF CAUTION

Just because locally grown and organic foods are better for the environment doesn't mean they're always healthier for our bodies. Locally grown, organic sugar? Sorry, it's still sugar to your body.

Confusion and controversy surround many types of food. In the following sections we'll go a bit more in depth about the different food groups to help you make more informed choices when ordering off a menu.

3

Everyone would be better off if a larger proportion of their diet consisted of plants—mostly vegetables (in particular, leafy greens), along with some nuts, seeds and fruits.

OK, so you've heard this many times before and still can't help but snooze when you hear "Eat more plants"? Maybe telling yourself "I'll have more energy" will provide the necessary motivation, because when we eat plant foods we are consuming the best energy there is.

To get this message to sink in, think about it in big, overarching terms. Eating plants is a way of taking in energy from the sun. As a life force, the sun makes an enormous contribution to our health and sense of well-being. Without it there would be no life on earth. Want more of it? Eat more plants. Unlike animal foods, plants are a direct source of "sun food."

If this concept is too esoteric, consider it from a scientific point of view. What gives green plants their color? It's chlorophyll, the pigment in leaves that enables them to absorb the sun's rays using a process called photosynthesis. Many nutritionists believe that when we eat green leaves, we take in that stored solar energy. Chlorophyll enriches blood, kills germs, detoxifies the bloodstream and liver, reduces bodily odors, and controls the appetite.

To help you navigate between different types of plants, the following two sections of this book are devoted to information about vegetables and fruits. It's not wrong to eat meat—in fact, it can be healthy—but eat lots of plants and you'll start to feel better. The next two sections show you why.

VEGGIE TALES

Pity the unappreciated vegetable. Perpetually shunted to the side—as a garnish, appetizer, side dish—it rarely gets to give all that it has to offer. What does it offer, you ask? An enormous amount of nutrients and health-boosting properties in the form of vitamins, minerals, fiber, phytochemicals and antioxidants. Vegetables should form the bulk of your diet.

THINK ABOUT IT:
YET ANOTHER REASON
TO EAT VEGGIES

Have you ever heard of anyone being overweight or getting heart disease or cancer from eating too many vegetables?

QUICK DEFINITION: ANTIOXIDANTS

Their name says it all: they're anti-oxidants. They counteract oxidation and the free radicals believed to speed up aging and disease. A variety of elements cause our bodies to produce excess free radicals, ranging from toxic air and the chemicals to which we're exposed, to the normal process of metabolizing food for energy. Fortunately, you can combat these excess free radicals by eating more vegetables (as well as fruits, nuts and seeds), which are abundant in antioxidants.

If you're a vegetarian, aim to increase the proportion of veggies that you consume relative to the amount of grains, beans, dairy, sugar and tofu in your diet. Similarly, omnivores should be mindful of the meat-to-vegetable ratio in each meal.

TIP: CROWD OUT THE BAD STUFF

The concept is simple: The more vegetables we eat, the less room we'll have for junk foods and the like. Just one extra helping of veggies a day crowds out one helping of unhealthy food, a fact that proves motivating when making dietary changes. Instead of trying to avoid bad foods, focus on eating more vegetables. You'll actually start craving them. Meanwhile, the junk will slowly become less appealing.

Remember to eat high-quality, natural and whole vegetables. They taste noticeably better, and local, organic vegetables tend to reap the benefits of healthier soils as well as suffer less nutrient loss than their long-distance counterparts.

To help you order at restaurants, here's a roundup of the types of vegetables you're likely to encounter on menus—and how they affect your body:

GREENS should be a priority because they're among the most nutrient-dense foods. Chock-full of chlorophyll, they also boast a calcium-to-magnesium ratio that makes them great bone builders and encourages relaxation and appropriate nerve-and-muscle responsiveness, ensuring the body's smooth functioning. They are also a good way to obtain iron, vitamin C and folate. Let's take a look at some of the more common leafy greens:

Kale, swiss chard, collards and spinach are all chef favorites. If possible, ask for yours to be lightly steamed or even served raw, both options that retain more nutrients than a long sauté. A quick sauté with olive oil and garlic is another delicious and healthy alternative. Spinach is probably the most familiar of leafy greens (thanks, Popeye!) but we encourage you to incorporate all types of leafy greens into your diet as spinach contains oxalic acid which some research shows could prevent proper nutrient absorption (but not enough that we recommend you avoid it all together).

Lettuce, mesclun greens, watercress and arugula often appear in salads and are a great way to get your raw-food fill. Watercress in particular is rich in B vitamins.

Parsley and dandelion greens, both highly nutritious, don't make it onto menus as often as other greens, except as a garnish. If you do see them on the menu, try them. They are both incredibly rich in vitamin K and vitamin C, and great for liver and kidney health.

Wheatgrass tends to conjure up images of earthy-crunchy types, but its health benefits beg you to look past this visual. It boasts one of the most concentrated sources of chlorophyll, a pigment (as you may recall from earlier) that captures the sun's energy and passes its healthful effects along to your body. Visit a juice bar (see p. 173) or health food restaurant and knock it back like a shot of the finest tequila.

CRUCIFEROUS VEGETABLES are plants in the cabbage family, a category that includes, to name a few, broccoli, cauliflower, Brussels sprouts, kale, bok choy and all cabbages (yes, there's some overlap with the leafy greens group). High in vitamin C and soluble fiber, these foods also are crammed with nutrients boasting potent anti-cancer properties. They are especially high in vitamin K, which plays an important role in the inflammation response. Only cruciferous vegetables contain isothiocyanates, nutrients that have been associated with a decrease in cancer.

ROOT VEGETABLES include carrots, beets, potatoes, parsnips, yams, turnips and radishes, each with a unique nutritional profile. Carrots and sweet potatoes, for instance, contain the antioxidant betacarotene, which helps prevent against free radicals; beets contain betalain, a unique antioxidant that acts as an anti-inflammatory and nurtures eye health and nerve tissue support.

> **TIP: THE INSTA-NUTRIENT SHOT**
>
> Drinking the juice of any type of green—not just wheatgrass—is a speedy way to get a nutrient infusion without your teeth or digestive system having to work at breaking down the plants' cell walls. Nevertheless, don't stop eating whole greens, since they provide fiber as well as some nutrients that may be lost or oxidized in the juicing process.

MUSHROOMS, which are actually fungi, not vegetables, probably generate the most controversy, at least as far as their health claims go. Some nutritionists advise steering clear because they are, after all, a type of fungus, and are therefore potentially infectious. They're also hard to digest when consumed raw. Other experts, however, particularly those who study Asian cultures, vaunt the medicinal properties of mushrooms. We suggest sticking with the shiitake and maitake (hen of the woods) varieties, both of which have cancer-fighting and immune-boosting properties. (Recent studies suggest that portobella mushrooms may lead to weight loss, and button mushrooms contain several goodies such as antioxidants, too.)

KIMCHI AND SAUERKRAUT are both raw and fermented veggies—the former served in Korean establishments and the latter in Eastern European restaurants. Literally "alive," they teem with nutrients, enzymes and probiotics, which aid digestion.

QUICK DEFINITION: PROBIOTICS AND ENZYMES

We hear it constantly: Such-and-such food boasts enzymes and probiotics. But what do those odd-sounding things do? Enzymes control the rate of every chemical reaction in your system, which means that you need them to digest food. So what happens when we don't get our enzymes, which are potentially destroyed by overcooking? Bad digestion. Probiotics are microorganisms that promote the growth of healthy bacteria in the gut that rid your intestines of the bad stuff. The upshot? You're healthier when you get probiotics.

SEAWEEDS, OR SEA VEGGIES, include nori (used to wrap sushi), hijiki, wakame, dulse and many others. Extremely dense in minerals, they add a salty, ocean-like taste to dishes and can often be found at Asian establishments and vegetarian eateries. Not familiar with this food? Try a seaweed salad or ask for extra in your miso soup; both are easy, delicious ways to familiarize yourself with sea veggies—and to enjoy a big, healthy dose of minerals.

THE RAINBOW RULE

It can be difficult to make sure you're getting the right balance of nutrients. Here's a good rule to follow: Eat as many different colors of vegetables each day as possible. Each pigment correlates to specific phytochemicals, all of which boost your immunity and act as health insurance against a range of nutrient deficiencies and diseases.

FEELING FRUITY

Think of fruits as sweets that are good for us! Fruits are good sources of fiber, antioxidants, phytochemicals and vitamins, and provide energy via easily digestible sugars. And don't be concerned about creating huge spikes in blood sugar; it's generally not an issue because fruits come packaged with fiber and other co-factors.

QUICK DEFINITION:

Co-factor: A co-factor is a nutrient that helps another nutrient work better.

As they should comprise a smaller percentage of your overall plant intake, it's fitting that fruit makes up a smaller percentage of plant foods offered at restaurants—vegetables pop up all over menus, but fruits tend to appear only in juices, smoothies or desserts.

Here are details about fruits you're likely to find on menus:

NON-SWEET FRUITS, such as peppers, tomatoes and cucumbers, rank low on the glycemic index and therefore barely disrupt our blood-sugar balance. During the summer, check out the many delicious varieties of locally grown heirloom tomatoes.

FATTY FRUITS, such as avocadoes and olives, are arguably the best

This system is a way of
ranking a food's effect on
your body's blood sugar
level. Using the numbers
1 through 100, the lower
the number, the lesser
the impact and the lower
the chance of unhealthy
blood-sugar spikes.

QUICK TIP: SQUEEZE
SOME LEMON IN YOUR
WATER

Even though lemons taste
acidic, they're actually
one of the most alkalizing
foods as far as the
chemistry they produce
in your blood. So squeeze
some lemon in your
morning glass of water
for an alkalizing start to
your day.

source of fats you can eat, because they are whole and come from plants (in contrast to many processed oils). Eaten raw, as they always should be, avocadoes and olives contain a fat-digesting enzyme, lipase, that makes them easy for our bodies to process.

BERRIES are a favorite sweet fruit, both from a culinary and nutritional perspective. On the glycemic index, they rank lowest of all the sweet fruits. Individually, each berry is touted for a specific attribute. For instance, blueberries offer significantly more vitamin K, while raspberries help to nourish the female reproductive system and provide fiber.

CITRUS FRUITS include oranges, lemons, limes and grapefruits. They tend to be high in immune-boosting vitamin C and in bioflavonoids—a type of antioxidant known for its anti-cancer properties, as well as its role in keeping blood capillaries healthy. Although citrus fruits taste acidic, they are, in fact, alkalizing and help to counteract the acidity of the meat, grains and beans that typically form the bulk of a restaurant meal.

ACID VS. ALKALINE

Let's travel back in time to your fifth grade science class. Remember learning about pH levels? A 7 on the 0-to-14 pH scale is neutral, with anything below considered acidic and anything above alkaline. Why is this relevant? Different foods create different byproducts in the metabolic process. Some foods, like animal products and processed foods, tend to cause more acidic residues, whereas others, like certain fruits and vegetables, create more alkaline residues. An acidic environment decreases the body's ability to absorb certain minerals and nutrients, inhibits the repair of damaged cells, causes inflammation, and hinders detoxification. Therefore, we want to consume less of the foods that create acidic residues and more of the foods that create alkaline residues for an optimal blood pH level.

ORCHARD FRUITS include apples, pears and peaches. Best eaten raw for their enzymes, fiber and nutrients, these fruits usually show up in fruit salads and smoothies.

TROPICAL FRUITS like papayas, mangoes and pineapples are especially rich in the kinds of enzymes that are not only powerful aids to digestion but also may help to break down scar tissue and waste materials in the body. They offer a tasty alternative to refined sugar for someone craving a sweet snack.

GRAINS

Many people consider a fresh-baked loaf of bread, or pasta with tomatoes and garlic, a bit of an indulgence—OK when eaten infrequently, but to be avoided in large quantities. And we agree. If you tolerate them well, grains can add fiber, protein, other nutrients and enjoyment to your diet, as long as they're properly prepared, eaten in moderation, not refined (soon to be explained) and organic (many grains are heavily sprayed and genetically modified).

That's not to say there aren't drawbacks. In fact, avoiding the complimentary bread basket served before most meals is recommended. Why? The body treats refined grains like sugar, upsetting your blood-sugar balance and contributing to weight gain and insulin resistance. In addition, unless grains are soaked or sprouted, their bran layer will contain phytic acid, which reduces mineral absorption and acts as an enzyme inhibitor, which interferes with digestion. And, overall, grains cause the body to produce mucus.

Grains are refined when their bran and germ layers are removed.

Grains are refined by
removing the bran (the
outer layer) and the germ,
the two most nutrient-rich
parts of grain. While the
fiber and nutrients are lost,
the calories stay intact. This
is why brown rice is usually
preferable to white.

The name of this substance
comes from the latin for
"glue," and, indeed, gluten
is responsible for the elastic,
stretchy quality of dough.
It's a mixture of two proteins
found in wheat and several
other grains, and it's a
common cause of allergies,
nutritional deficiencies and
serious digestive complaints.
While there are varying
degrees of intolerance to
gluten, it's quite likely that
many people are somewhat
sensitive to it and would
be better off reducing their
gluten intake.

They are further refined when they're milled into flour for breads and pasta. In fact, white wheat flour is one of the worst of the refined grains. It has a high gluten content, few nutrients and it's usually adulterated with bleaching agents and other chemicals to enhance its performance. Unfortunately, refined wheat flour is used in a whopping 90 percent of baked goods. Additionally, flour is prone to rancidity, and it causes a big, unhealthy spike in blood sugar levels (because the fiber isn't there to slow down the release of glucose).

Preparation techniques make a big difference as well; traditional methods yield more-nutritious, easier-to-digest dishes. When possible, opt for sprouted grains. These have been soaked in water until germination occurs, thereby neutralizing the grain's phytic acid content and increasing the availability of its nutrients. You can now find sprouted breads at health-focused eateries.

Sourdough is another smart choice since it's naturally leavened with a traditional fermentation technique that offers the same benefits of sprouting and creates lactobacillus—a probiotic that aids digestion.

To sum up: Say yes to moderation, traditional preparation methods and whole grains— and no to refined, milled and non-organic versions. An overview of key grains follows. They are divided into gluten grains and non-gluten grains for people who are allergic or sensitive. Even if you aren't, cutting down on gluten may be good for your health.

GLUTEN GRAINS

WHEAT is highest in gluten of all the grains, which is why it's the universal choice for bread-making. Gluten helps bread to rise. It's also the main ingredient in most pasta, pizza crusts, pastries, crackers, cakes and cookies, and is even used as a thickener in sauces. Incidentally, seitan—a popular meat substitute for vegetarians and vegans—is essentially wheat gluten with the texture of meat, so go easy on it if you are concerned about gluten.

BULGUR AND COUSCOUS are hybrids of different wheat species. Used like rice, bulgur is a staple in Middle Eastern restaurants and is best known as the main ingredient in tabbouleh. Couscous is typically found in North African and Moroccan cuisine. Bulgur is a whole grain as the bran and germ are still intact; couscous is not.

KAMUT AND SPELT are naturally hybridized, ancient varieties of wheat. Kamut is actually the brand name for khorasan wheat. Because they have a different form of gluten than wheat, and are more nutritious, both make good substitutes. In fact, you may do well with spelt even if you're sensitive to gluten due to the difference in gluten composition. Health-focused eateries now offer spelt-based options.

RYE, rich in a variety of nutrients, is used in place of wheat in items like rye bread and German pumpernickel. Many delis, diners and sandwich shops offer rye or pumpernickel options.

BARLEY is one of the most ancient cultivated grains and is said to be soothing to the intestines. Typically restaurants will use pearled barley to make risotto. Opt for hulled barley when possible, as it is the most whole form.

NON-GLUTEN GRAINS

RICE is one of the richest sources of B vitamins and is served at all

TIP: AL DENTE PASTA

Al dente is the best option for cooked pasta because it has a softer impact on blood sugar levels; overcooked pasta causes a more rapid spike.

types of restaurants. As discussed above, brown rice is a more whole option. Black and wild rice are also good choices.

CORN today often comes from genetically modified crops, so always ask if it is organic. Many Mexican establishments use corn flour as the base for tortillas and arepas.

OATS stabilize blood sugar, reduce cholesterol, and soothe the intestines and nervous system. Not usually encountered at dinner, oat-based dishes like oatmeal, granola and muesli are common breakfast offerings. Oats also appear in some baked goods. Opt for steel-cut oats when possible, as they are the most whole form. Many restaurant chains are now incorporating steel-cut oats in their breakfast menus. Some oats may be processed with gluten. Be sure to check that the label says "gluten-free."

BUCKWHEAT is one of only a few commercial crops not routinely sprayed with pesticides, because it has its own natural resistance. With the longest gut transit time of all the grains, it is the most filling and stabilizing for blood sugar levels. Buckwheat flour is often used to make pancakes, and soba noodles at Japanese restaurants, while buckwheat groats, the most whole form, is often used in Russian cuisine (called kasha) and some granolas.

QUINOA, technically a seed, was a major staple for the Incas of South America. Its high protein content, mild taste and fluffy texture have made it enormously popular. Quinoa can now be spotted on menus across multiple cuisines.

AMARANTH is not as widely available in restaurants as other grains, but it is becoming increasingly popular due to its nutrition profile. Amaranth contains unique essential amino acids such as lysine, which is important for maintaining bone, cholesterol and heart health.

MILLET is another excellent option. While perhaps best known as birdseed in the U.S., this cereal grass is popular in Asian and African cuisine. It is easily digested and very nutritious, with a high silica content for healthy skin and bones.

LEGUMES

They're the punch line of bad jokes, true, but beans—as well as peas and lentils—confer many health benefits. Known as legumes, or pulses, they lower cholesterol, control blood-sugar imbalances and regulate bowel functions. Low in fat (with the exception of soy beans), they're a good source of vegetarian protein, fiber and B vitamins. From a culinary perspective, herbs and spices marry well with the mild taste of legumes, which absorb the flavor of sauces and have a pleasant texture that adds bulk to any meal.

For a few susceptible individuals, abdominal gas and bloating result from eating beans, no matter how carefully they are prepared. But most of us need not avoid beans for fear of their antisocial effects. A good chef knows that most varieties of beans should be presoaked, rinsed and thoroughly cooked to break down their indigestible sugars and destroy their enzyme inhibitors (if they haven't come from a can).

Here's the dish on beans:

CHICKPEAS, BLACK BEANS, KIDNEY BEANS, ADZUKI BEANS AND LENTILS crop up in numerous cultures, where they have nourished humankind for millennia. Chickpeas, also called garbanzo beans, are used to make the hummus and falafels of Mediterranean cuisine and are popular in Indian curries; black beans are used in Mexican burritos; kidney beans are the legume of choice for chili; the adzuki bean is popular in macrobiotic restaurants; and red lentils often form the basis of dhal (dal, daal, dahl), an easily digested Indian puree.

SOY BEANS merit a lengthier discussion because they're eaten so frequently and used in so many ways—and, in particular, associated with numerous health claims and controversies.

Asians have been including soy foods in their diets for thousands of years, a fact that's often touted as the main reason for Asians' longevity and low rates of certain cancers and other Western diseases. However, this may have more to do with the paucity of dairy and meat in the Asian diet, as well as the emphasis on vegetables and various lifestyle factors. The truth is that soy has never been eaten in large quantities in Asia. Note the miso soup in Japanese restaurants, in which only a few cubes of tofu float around. And the next time you order Chinese vegetables with soy-bean curd, observe how the vegetables and rice predominate. This marginal role for soy stands in stark contrast to the modern soy burger at the center of the vegetarian entrée. Over the past few decades, vegetarians and vegans in particular have become over-reliant on soy because it is a balanced protein and can be formed into mock meat products.

However, studies detailing soy's high nutrient content and positive effects have recently been contested by additional research. Soy is known to block the absorption of some nutrients and is thought to increase the likelihood of ovarian and breast cancer.

One solution is simply to cut back. Another is to be mindful of the kinds of soy products you consume. Organic, non-GMO soy is your best bet, as are soy products like miso, soy yogurt, natto and tempeh, all of which undergo a fermentation process in which otherwise non-viable nutrients are partly predigested—and phytates and enzyme inhibitors that cause gastric distress are neutralized. In addition, these forms of soy are endowed with probiotics. With the possible exception of soy yogurt, these healthy forms of soy are usually available in Chinese, Japanese and macrobiotic restaurants.

Tofu, perhaps the most ubiquitous form of soy in restaurants, provides some nutrition but should be eaten in moderation since it hasn't undergone the all-important fermentation process.

As for edamame, it's a whole food but not easy to digest—good for you, but not in excess.

Soy milk, soy ice cream and soy cheese, however, are highly processed and not fermented—best consumed only on occasion. They usually come with additives of one kind or another in an attempt to mimic the flavor and texture of the real thing.

TVP (textured vegetable or soy protein), which in similar forms goes by the names protein soy isolate or hydrolyzed plant (or soy) protein, should be completely avoided whenever possible. It is made from soybean meal after the oil has been processed out with chemicals and intense pressure. These soy products are typically used in veggie burgers and fake meat products. They bear a close chemical resemblance to plastic and may contain residues from processing, including petroleum solvents, sulfuric acids, hydrochloric acid and caustic soda. Those are just a few good reasons to bypass that fake turkey sandwich in favor of the tempeh Reuben.

#4

If you choose to eat animal products, consume only (a) high-quality and sustainably raised animals (ideally pasture-raised and grass-fed, but at least hormone- and antibiotic-free); and do so (b) in moderation—meaning smaller portions with less frequency.

Meat still enjoys a reputation as being as all-American as the Wild West and cowboy boots. But self-improvement is an all-American quality, too, and to do that it's best to cut down on your intake of animal products, including meat, poultry, dairy and eggs. This does not mean you have to become vegetarian or vegan. Each individual should do what's best for his or her body.

Remember how proponents of *The China Study* argue that meat eating is a leading cause of human disease, while followers of the nutritionist Weston A. Price say it is beneficial? That's not the only area of contention regarding animal products.

Another is whether animal fats cause heart disease. An increasingly vocal minority of researchers claim the cholesterol myth is just that—a myth. They believe that highly processed vegetable oils and hydrogenated fats are more artery-clogging and lead to more heart trouble than lard. Of course, adherents of veganism and vegetarianism eschew animal products for a variety of reasons, while others believe that those diets are lacking in essential nutrients such as vitamins B12 and D. Different people will side with different research; your genetic makeup or lifestyle may mean that eating meat is necessary for your body to function smoothly. To figure it out, experiment and think about how certain foods and dietary principles make you feel.

If you consume animal products, do so in moderation. Why? For one thing, eating too many provides more protein than necessary for human health, creating more acidity than the body can process and leading to problems like fatigue and osteoporosis. In addition, there's substantial evidence that the practice of raising animals for human consumption—especially in conventional corporate feedlots—is unsustainable and environmentally problematic. Easy ways to lower the percentage of animal products in your diet include thinking of meat as a side dish rather than a main course, as well as eating smaller portions and less frequently.

In addition, make sure that all the animal products you consume—beef, dairy, eggs, chicken and so on—come from high-quality, organic and pasture-fed animals. Animal products are a concentrated source of the medications, stress, hormones and environmental toxins that the animal has been exposed to. This is a good reason to steer clear of factory-farmed animals. Jammed together in pens where they never see sunlight and are injected with hormones and who knows what else, these animals are often very sick—part of the reason they're injected with excess antibiotics. That's a powerful argument for choosing an organic, pasture-fed animal, which won't have been subjected to stressful conditions or injected with toxins. Instead, it will have been raised similarly to the way it would have been in the wild. A pasture-raised cow, for instance, grazes on grass, gets exercise and is exposed to the sun, all of which results in a healthy cow—and extra benefits for us.

Please note, organic and grass-fed are not the same thing. While organic does ensure minimal to no use of excess hormones and antibiotics, they are still fed grains, corn or organic vegetarian feed. Often, this is for taste reasons, but sometimes, even these animals are purposefully overfed—a practice that makes them more desirable in the market but also more prone to disease. Since grass is the natural diet for most animals, animals that eat grains or corn—even if it's high-quality, organic—are not as healthy as their grass-fed counterparts and therefore not as healthy for humans.

THINK ABOUT IT: FACTORY-FARMED COWS AND OBESITY

To make more money, growth hormones are injected into factory-farmed animals, so each animal's cells contain these hormones. When we consume meat, we are eating the cells of the animal—and the growth hormones contained therein. Perhaps that's one of the reasons we are facing an epidemic of obesity?

COOKING METHODS MATTER

In addition to knowing where your animal products have come from, it is also important to prepare them properly. For instance, grilled or roasted meats are better for you than deep-fried dishes. Be aware, though: Meats smoked or barbecued on charcoal grills can develop a carcinogen called polycyclic aromatic hydrocarbons. Like most other foods, meat is best for your body when it has been cooked briefly and gently. Prolonged high heat reduces the amount of vitamins and minerals in meat and denatures its protein. Worse, it increases the toxicity of contaminants already there, such as nitrates and pesticides. Of course, with so many disease-causing pathogens showing up in animal products, it may not be such a bad idea to avoid rare or raw meat (which otherwise would be the healthiest way to consume high-quality, properly raised animal products). However, when possible, ask that your meat not be overcooked. Medium-rare is a good option and usually what chefs prefer anyway.

REMINDER: DON'T NECESSARILY WORRY ABOUT ORGANIC CERTIFICATION

Small farmers who raise animals sustainably and without the use of antibiotics or hormones often can't afford to obtain the "certified organic" accreditation.

Not all foods can be properly digested when eaten together. Concentrated starches and proteins, for instance, should be eaten separately, as protein causes the body to produce specific enzymes and hydrochloric acid, which increases the stomach's acidity. This makes it more difficult to digest starch.

Translation: Eating a lot of meat with starches like bread or potatoes can cause gas and indigestion. A food-combining solution: Pair heavy proteins like meat with vegetables, such as leafy greens, instead of with starches like breads, grains and potatoes.

To summarize: Make sure that the animal products you eat are high-quality and organic (that is, hormone- and antibiotic-free), and preferably grass-fed. In addition, consume them less often and in small portions—and eat them with vegetables (especially leafy greens) to counteract some of the potential negative effects. Order your meat medium-rare whenever possible. By making these tweaks to your diet, you ensure that high-quality meat, fish, poultry, dairy and eggs can become a healthy part of a balanced diet rather than a risk factor.

Here are details about the different types of meats you're likely to encounter on menus:

BEEF is a source of iron and vitamin B12, as well as essential fats. Cows raised in pastures—where they're exposed to the sun and eat grass—provide the healthiest meat; in fact, an anti-cancer nutrient called conjugated linoleic acid (CLA) occurs only in grass-fed animals.

CHICKEN, LAMB AND PORK, all sources of complete protein, can be good for you, like beef, if you choose an organic, naturally raised animal and eat it in moderation. When it comes to pork, though, don't be fooled by the advertising "The Other White Meat." It's probably less healthy for you than chicken or lamb. Above all, it makes such a difference to your health that we'll repeat: Order free-range, naturally fed chicken, lamb or pork—and consume small portions.

GAME ANIMALS like bison and venison are among the healthiest kinds of meats because most often they come from freshly killed animals that lived in the wild. These animals are leaner than beef and boast a higher proportion of omega-3 fatty acids. In addition, they're less likely to be contaminated or diseased. It is becoming easier to find bison and venison in trendy restaurants, as well as establishments emphasizing organic dishes, although, for some, venison's gamey flavor is an acquired taste.

CURED MEATS like sausages, luncheon meats and bacon can be OK in moderation; it all comes down to how they are raised and made. I recommend cutting out luncheon meats altogether—nearly all of them contain carcinogenic preservatives such as nitrates. But if you can't stay away from, say, bologna, at least opt for nitrate-free varieties. Two requirements should be met before you purchase bacon or sausage: (1) The meat should have come from a good-quality animal, and (2) the way the meat was made should be as natural as possible. Sausage without casings or fillers, produced on the premises at an organic restaurant, for instance, gets a thumbs-up—as long as you eat it in moderation.

> **INTERESTING TIDBIT: ORGAN MEATS**
>
> A few nutritionally minded types, including followers of Weston A. Price, believe that the healthiest parts of an animal to eat are its organs, like the liver, as long as it comes from a properly raised animal. (When we consume meat we tend to eat steak, which is a muscle.)

FOIE GRAS AND VEAL tend to be served only in upscale restaurants. The former is the liver of a fattened-up goose or duck, and the latter is the meat of a milk-fed (or sometimes formula-fed) baby calf. A lot of people avoid veal and foie gras (French for "fat liver") for moral reasons. Since they don't provide any particular health benefits, it's best avoiding them altogether.

COLD-WATER FISH like salmon, mackerel, cod and sardines are

chock-full of heart-healthy omega-3 fatty acids as well as fat-soluble vitamins and minerals, including iodine. Unfortunately, these benefits are minimized if the fish is conventionally farm-raised, a technique that results in more PCBs, mercury and disease—and fewer omega-3s. Plus, the feed for farmed salmon usually contains dye to give the flesh a pink color.

If you want the benefits of organically farm-raised or wild fish, salmon is probably the easiest fish to find at restaurants. Most nutritious in its raw form (for instance, as sashimi), it's also healthy when steamed or baked. Skip tempura, though; it involves dipping the fish in batter before deep-frying in hot oil.

SCAVENGER FISH include tuna, swordfish, carp and catfish. They eat almost anything they find in the sea, including dead fish (yum!). That's why their tissues are likely to contain the toxins of other fish, like PCBs and mercury; it's also why scavenger fish are considered no-no's for women who are pregnant or breastfeeding. If you like fish, stick mostly to the cold-water kind.

SHELLFISH like scallops, clams, mussels, oysters, shrimp, crabs and lobsters should be eaten in moderation and only while very fresh and in season. Shellfish spoil easily and are a common cause of food poisoning, as well as being prone to contamination. Be sure yours are sourced from clean waters.

To help you make quality seafood choices while dining out, download the Monterey Bay Aquarium's Seafood Watch mobile app. It lists fish both high in omega-3 fatty acids and low in environmental contaminants.

DAIRY AND EGGS

MILK'S big selling point is that it's a source of calcium. Yet research shows that milk's acidity means it can actually leach calcium from our bones. In addition, milk's low magnesium content relative to its calcium content means our bodies may not be able to benefit from milk's calcium, as they are required to be in balance for proper utilization. Calcium is better obtained from vegetables, seeds and nuts. Many people are lactose intolerant; only a third of the world's population possesses the genetic mutation required for the proper digestion of dairy. Populations from Asian and African descent have an especially high percentage of milk-intolerant individuals, which is why you're not likely to find many dairy products on their menus.

This doesn't mean milk is the devil, at least not for people who digest it well—as long as you get it from grass-fed cows, or at minimum, opt for an organic version. Avoiding products containing Recombinant Bovine Growth Hormone (aka RBGH), a genetically engineered drug associated with growth abnormalities and malignant tumors, is recommended. Another reason to go organic: Dairy cows fed unnatural diets, forced to produce excessive quantities of milk, and confined to small stalls or kept in unhygienic conditions often suffer from infected udders. This infection, called mastitis, causes the sick cows to release pus into their milk.

CHEESE can be enjoyed as part of a wholesome meal so long as it is from an organic, grass-fed source. Raw cheeses tend to preserve the most nutrients. Sheep and goat cheeses are another smart alternative. They are easier to digest than cheese made from cow's milk. These cheeses are increasingly popular in restaurants, where you might find them atop salads and as sandwich fillings. Avoid processed cheese, a staple in sandwich shops, delis, and fast-food entrées; they usually contain additives such as emulsifiers, extenders, phosphates and hydrogenated oils. You'll likely find them easy to give up, considering their bland taste and plastic texture.

CULTURED DAIRY PRODUCTS like kefir, yogurt and sour cream are easier to digest than other dairy items because their lactose and casein are already partially broken down. Kefir (a fermented yogurt drink) and yogurt also supply some healthy gut-promoting probiotics.

BUTTER most often appears at your table accompanying that insidious complimentary bread basket. Unless you have a dairy allergy, a moderate amount of butter—especially organic, from grass-fed cows—offers some benefits, including easily digested fats and the fat-soluble vitamins A and D.

EGGS are rich in vitamins, minerals and protein, and can be quite nourishing. Their cholesterol content, however, causes debate. When overcooked, the yolk becomes oxidized, meaning it transforms from a useful nutrient into a potentially harmful chemical. For that reason, avoid powdered eggs, which have been through a heating and drying process and therefore contain oxidized cholesterol. To avoid oxidation, order lightly poached or sunny-side-up eggs rather than scrambled or fried; similarly, soft-boiled trumps hard-boiled. Raw eggs are even more beneficial than the lightly cooked kind, although people susceptible to salmonella, such as the elderly, the infirm or pregnant women, should avoid them.

TIP: EAT THE WHOLE EGG

The yolk contains a good deal of nutrients the white doesn't provide, like anti-inflammatory choline and antioxidant lutein. Plus, the yolk promotes a healthy HDL/LDL cholesterol ratio. So eat the whole shebang, yolk and white. Your body will thank you.

As with dairy and meat, a chef's choice of egg supplier has implications for both nutritional quality and taste. Battery-caged hens are more likely to turn out eggs with salmonella, fewer nutrients and a bland or fishy taste—and the cruelty of crowding hens together is another reason to skip ordering such eggs. Free-range, pasture-raised hens, on the other hand, produce eggs with richer flavor and increased nutrient content. At the very least, stick with hormone- and antibiotic-free eggs taken from cage-free hens.

#5

To feel better immediately, simply reduce your intake of artificial, chemical-laden processed foods as well as refined sugar and poor-quality oils.

THIS SECTION IS all about the food that makes your mouth water: sweeteners, seasonings, fats and oils, and beverages. While generally thought of as harmful, they don't have to be, as long as you approach these full-of-flavor foods the right way.

FATS AND OILS

They've got a less-than-savory rep, but don't be afraid of fats and oils. They play an important role in the human diet.

Fats slow the release of sugar from other foods, create a feeling of satisfaction, give us a source of energy, and allow us to absorb fat-soluble vitamins A, D, E and K by carrying them across the gut wall. In addition, our bodies use fats as building materials, incorporating them into cell membranes to create the right balance between firmness and flexibility.

We like to preach about its evils—weight gain, heart disease—while still associating fatty food with comfort and fun. The truth is, it can get complicated, so let's simplify. The list of different fats and oils is a long one, so here's what you need to know about the ones you are most likely to encounter at a restaurant.

TRANS FATS or hydrogenated oils, made by injecting hydrogen into liquid vegetable oils to make them more solid, should be completely avoided as they are probably the most harmful ingredient in our food supply. In fact, New York City has ensured you'll avoid these oils because in 2008 the city banned the use of trans fats in restaurants, so it is far less likely than before that dining out will mean consuming damaged vegetable oils in the form of vegetable shortening and hydrogenated margarine.

VEGETABLE OILS like soybean and canola are the most commonly used cooking and frying oils and should be avoided as much as possible as they are usually made from GMO crops, are highly processed and lead to inflammation and a host of other ailments.

COCONUT OIL provides a unique medium chained fat that is easily burned for energy instead of stored in the body. It is also a source of lauric acid, which has anti-bacterial and anti-viral properties. More and more restaurants are now using coconut oil to prepare foods thanks to its ability to withstand higher temperatures and the many health benefits it provides. Try coconut meat as well—juice bars will often offer both coconut meat and oil as add-ins for smoothies.

HEMPSEED AND FLAXSEED are valued for their essential fatty acids, but they are best used whole and raw, since processing, storage and heating can turn these delicate oils rancid. They contain high levels of omega-3 (minus contaminants such as mercury and PCBs). It's best to eat the seeds ground. Hemp and flax oils are healthy only when cold-pressed; in that form they make excellent salad dressings. They are not suitable for cooking or baking.

THE PROS AND CONS OF FLAX

Flaxseed is known for being an excellent vegetarian source not only of omega-3 fatty acids but also of calcium, iron and vitamin E. However, the type of omega-3s flax provides is not the same as the type fish provides. That's why, if you're not a vegetarian, it's best to incorporate wild or organically farmed fish into your diet in addition to flaxseed.

Most restaurants use
inflammatory refined
vegetable oils for cooking.
Well-sourced ghee, lard and
coconut oil are fats stable
enough to withstand higher
temperatures without too
many free radicals being
formed in the process. Ask
your restaurant what they
use for cooking.

OLIVE OIL is a monounsaturated fat. Even though it has negligible amounts of essential fatty acids, it's better than many other oils as it provides a good source of oleic acid, which can help stabilize blood sugar levels. To receive the most benefits, opt for extra-virgin, cold-pressed, organic olive oil and consume unheated when possible—for example, as a salad dressing or drizzled over veggies.

BUTTER has become cool again after the downfall of margarine because of its dangerous levels of trans fats (hydrogenated oils). As explained above, butter—especially organic butter from a grass-fed cow—has some health benefits when consumed in moderation. Margarine, on the other hand, can damage your arteries more than any amount of butterfat because of its aforementioned trans fats. Its overuse in recent years—along with oils like soy, sunflower and corn—has contributed to a national over-consumption of omega-6 fatty acids, a situation that has been linked to numerous health problems.

GHEE is a clarified butter—meaning the milk solids have been removed, so even those who are lactose intolerant may be able to digest it.

SALT AND SEASONINGS

Salt is our main source of sodium, an important mineral involved in many bodily processes. Our bodies rely on a balanced ratio of potassium (a mineral found mainly in fresh fruits and veggies) and sodium for the smooth functioning of our muscles, lungs, heart and nervous system, as well as for the water balance within our bodies. Most people get way more than enough sodium, as it is overabundant in our modern, processed meals—even restaurants tend to use too much. We need about one teaspoon of sodium per day, but many of us are consuming many times that amount. Potassium, however, is lacking because we don't eat enough fresh fruits and vegetables. Too much sodium can lead to raised blood pressure, muscle cramps and water retention.

Next time you dine out, request that your meal be prepared with less salt. You'll be amazed at how quickly you lose the desire for excess salt and start to find too much unappealing.

TIP: GOOD SALT SUBSTITUTES

One clever and healthful way to reduce your sodium intake at a restaurant is to ask for herbs or spices to be substituted instead, a move that will increase the flavor of your meal while adding health benefits. Some of the best additions are garlic, a natural antibiotic; ginger, which prevents against nausea; cayenne, a circulation enhancer; turmeric, an anti-inflammatory; and green herbs such as parsley or cilantro, good sources of vitamins and chlorophyll.

REFINED TABLE SALT tends to be processed and altered with chemicals—it's sodium chloride with no nutritional benefits. Delete it from your diet, since it contributes to the sodium-potassium imbalance described above and usually contains aluminum to boot.

KOSHER SALT is a coarse salt with no additives; its thick crystal grains help to cure meat and are used in the process of making meat kosher—thus its name. Foodies like this salt for its texture and taste. Perhaps because it appears in gourmet foods, it's sometimes thought to be healthier than table salt. That's not the case, however; there's no nutritional difference between table and kosher salt. The latter may be marginally more healthful because it doesn't have additives, but don't be fooled into thinking it's good for you.

SEA SALT OR HIMALAYAN CRYSTAL SALT both appear at some restaurants and are fine to eat in moderation. Natural and unprocessed, they contain minerals, have a better flavor than table salt and tend to be prized by top chefs. Although sea and crystal salt are gaining in popularity, they're still most likely to crop up only in the kitchens of health-food or gourmet restaurants. At raw-food restaurants, they're usually the only kind of salt offered.

SHOYU AND TAMARI, both commonly referred to as soy sauce, are more or less interchangeable; both are fermented soy condiments, except that tamari is wheat-free. Asian and health-food restaurants serve shoyu and tamari, where they're sometimes also used for stir-frying. Health-conscious diners prefer naturally brewed versions over highly processed and additive-laden cheaper imitations. However, soy sauce is a questionable substitute for table salt because of the soy, wheat and inevitable processing. Unless stated on the label, soy sauce is not a low-sodium alternative and is best used sparingly.

SWEETENERS

"You're sweet." "How sweet it is." "That's sweet." The English language is peppered with remarks about how sweet sweetness is. So it's understandable that sugary foods tend to illicit the most resistance and guilt from people.

It's not exactly a news flash that refined white sugar and the more insidious high-fructose corn syrup are bad for us. It's difficult to get away from, though, because sugar is in all kinds of foods—not just bottled drinks and desserts, but also packaged foods and savory sauces.

Even if we're aware of which foods contain refined white sugar, it's hard not to order them. That's because sugar is biologically and emotionally addictive. Stop eating it and you may experience withdrawal symptoms. Eat some and you will crave more. Consider how children are offered sweets if they're "good" or "behave." To make matters worse, it seems that we have been biologically programmed to seek out sweetness as a way to avoid poison, which tends to be bitter. But it's a safe bet that evolution intended for us to eat fruits rather than doughnuts.

Even though you know that sweets aren't good for you, it's worth pointing out the many ways they're bad. Sugar is an anti-nutrient, not only giving the body zero nutrition but actually robbing us of goodies. Plus, it's probably the major contributor to weight gain. At a certain point of saturation the body converts it to fat, putting excess sugar into storage in order to quickly remove it from the blood where it would otherwise create havoc. After all, there is only so much sugar that we can use as energy. Sugar has been linked to a variety of other ailments, from lowered immunity and poor gut flora to cancer and diabetes. Yet research at George Washington University shows that the average American consumes 30 teaspoons of sugar and sweeteners per day!

So what should we do? We have to be smart about our approach to sugar. Once you begin to take better care of yourself in other areas of your life and eat better-quality foods, your sugar cravings tend to lessen. Sometimes exercise helps, as does eating a bit more protein and drinking more water. And consider switching to more natural, gentler forms of sweeteners. Take these steps and over time you will gradually find that refined sugar actually tastes too sweet. True, it may take a while, but this approach can really work, even for the most avid sugar addict.

Let's take a look at some of the common sweeteners you will encounter at restaurants:

WHITE TABLE SUGAR, HIGH-FRUCTOSE CORN SYRUP AND EVEN BROWN SUGAR should be avoided as much as possible.

ORGANIC RAW CANE SUGAR, FLORIDA CRYSTALS AND TURBINADO SUGAR have gained in popularity and are commonly found on the tables and in desserts at health-food restaurants. These sugars are a slightly better option than the completely refined stuff since they retain some nutrients and are better for the environment, but they're not healthy.

MAPLE SYRUP AND BROWN RICE SYRUP are preferable to all the above. They are the most commonly consumed natural sweeteners. They are OK in moderation if they are pure and of a high quality. Maple syrup is a better option because it has a lower glycemic index and provides more minerals. (Please note: Aunt Jemima is not real maple syrup!)

RAW HONEY is a far better choice than many of the other sweeteners, as it is rich in antioxidants, enzymes and various healing co-factors.

RAW AGAVE NECTAR has its issues, including a very high fructose content and the likelihood of poor production quality. Use it in moderation from an organic source.

COCONUT PALM SUGAR is becoming a popular choice due to its low impact on blood sugar levels and its ability to retain minerals and phytonutrients during processing. It is still a sugar, though, so like all sweeteners it should be consumed in moderation.

STEVIA, extracted from the sweet leaves of the stevia plant, is also becoming increasingly popular for its sugary taste and safeness for diabetics, although some people are not crazy about its aftertaste. In addition, there is conflicting research regarding its safety.

ARTIFICIAL SWEETENERS like Splenda, Equal and NutraSweet (aspartame) should be avoided as there are many adverse reactions reported to the FDA. Plus, there is convincing evidence that these artificial sweeteners can still mess with insulin levels thus leading to weight gain.

BEVERAGES

A sparkling stream of water runs through a picturesque valley. This could be an ad for anything from beer to an energy drink. The point? Advertisers know that we know that water is good for us. So they use it to sell beverages that aren't so good. Read on for details about the drinks you'll find at restaurants.

WATER should be your beverage of choice, as it's the most natural and purest liquid you can get. In restaurants, bottled water tends to be overpriced, but it may be worth it if the only other option is tap water, which may be polluted by contaminants. Filtered tap water is the best option; it's free, safe and better for the environment than bottled water (plus, you avoid ingesting chemicals that may leach into the water from the plastic bottle). If the restaurant's water is filtered, the food that's cooked in it will be safer for you as well.

FRUIT JUICES are OK to drink but quite sugary and usually void of fiber. Try diluting them with water.

VEGETABLE JUICES are a better option. They count toward your nutrient intake, especially with dark greens thrown in.

SODAS AND SOFT DRINKS are composed of unfiltered, artificially carbonated water with added sugar (or, worse, corn syrup or artificial sweeteners), flavorings, colorings, preservatives and sometimes caffeine. In addition, their high phosphoric-acid content is associated with osteoporosis. Not a recipe for health. Avoid them altogether, especially the diet ones, which are loaded with artificial sweeteners that, research has suggested, actually may cause weight gain.

COFFEE can provide a much-needed lift. Still, it's best to reduce caffeine consumption. Sure, coffee beans may contain antioxidants; plus, some people metabolize caffeine better than others. However, caffeine in general, and coffee in particular, is linked to raised blood pressure, insomnia, nervous conditions, osteoporosis and certain

> **TIP: WATER TEMPERATURE**
>
> Room-temperature water is the healthiest kind. That's because cold water is difficult to digest, so ask for yours with no ice—but with a slice of lemon, which makes the water more alkalizing and cleansing.

> **TIP: ELECTROLYTES FOR ATHLETES**
>
> Looking to replenish those electrolytes after a tough workout? Replace your Gatorade with coconut water. It's loaded with electrolytes and a naturally sweet taste.

cancers. At the very least, drinking caffeine with your meal reduces the availability of minerals in the food—it leaches them out.

If you can't resist ordering a cup, check whether the restaurant offers an organic, fair-trade or shade-grown version.

TIP: COFFEE REPLACEMENT

Raw cacao beans, or nibs, make a tasty interim crutch for people trying to break their coffee habit. Cacao will give you a lift, partially from caffeine and partially from other natural, happiness-inducing chemicals. Plus, they are extraordinarily rich in magnesium and antioxidants. (Sorry, chocolate bars with their cooked cacao and sugar don't count as a whole-food alternative to coffee.) Some macrobiotic and health-focused restaurants will offer a grain coffee substitute, typically made from chicory. They are caffeine-free yet have coffee's robust taste.

GREEN TEA may be the most healthful, or at least the most benign, of all caffeinated beverages. That's because it contains polyphenols, a type of antioxidant that can reduce blood pressure (coffee's opposite effect), lower blood fats and combat those free radicals we encounter in a city environment. It contains much less caffeine than coffee. In addition, it has theanine, which mitigates some of caffeine's effects to produce a calmer type of energy and prevents a caffeine "hangover."

BLACK TEA has fewer antioxidants and more caffeine than green. But it doesn't contain as much caffeine as coffee unless it is steeped for an especially long time.

Both green and black teas come from the same plant, often one that's been heavily sprayed, so seek an organic version.

HERBAL TEAS may be the best hot drink overall, since they are naturally caffeine-free and boast mild therapeutic benefits. For instance, peppermint and ginger tea both are helpful to drink after a heavy meal, since they aid digestion; chamomile, as you probably know, has calming properties.

DECAFFEINATED COFFEE OR TEA is fine to drink if the caffeine has been removed using the Swiss-water process. Otherwise, residue from chemicals used to remove the caffeine might remain—a non-issue if the product is certified organic. And note that all decaffeinated beverages still contain some traces of caffeine.

FERMENTED DRINKS like amazake (made from rice), kefir (a lacto-fermented yogurt drink), traditional ginger ale, apple cider and kombucha (a fermented tea drink), are mostly found in health-focused restaurants. It may take a few tries to become accustomed to their tangy taste, but they are worth getting used to, as they are rich in enzymes and probiotics and aid in strong digestion.

WINE is fermented, true, but its alcohol content tends to neutralize the much-touted health benefits. Although some research may say that wine is good for you in various small ways, some people use that as an excuse to drink too much. Even in relatively small amounts, wine is an anti-nutrient, particularly good at robbing the body of B vitamins. All alcohol can make you accident prone, dehydrated, unable to concentrate and even aggressive. It should be avoided if you are susceptible to candida overgrowth. And it's worth repeating: Long-term drinking to excess, whether labeled alcoholism or not, can result in liver damage and stomach ulcers, not to mention a host of social and emotional problems.

Still, like coffee, alcohol can be useful in moderation. After a stressful day at work, a relaxing glass of wine can make all the difference to your enjoyment of a meal and your ability to converse with fellow diners. Plus, it can stimulate the digestive process. Red wine in particular provides some antioxidant benefits and is said to be good for the heart in moderate amounts. As with coffee, though, there is no need to rely on wine for your antioxidants; think vegetables and fruits instead. Opt for organic and/or biodynamic wines when possible as they are free of pesticides and the producers usually go to extraordinary lengths to create special, pure growing conditions. Also look for sulfite-free or NSA wines, meaning "no sulfites added." Sulfites occur naturally in grapes, but many vineyards add more to prevent bacterial growth, oxidation and a vinegary taste. Many people experience allergic side effects, including headaches, when they consume sulfites, and some connoisseurs prefer the taste of a low-sulfite wine. White wine generally has fewer sulfites than red.

BEER, ALE AND LAGER are lower in alcohol than wine, but it's still important to watch the amount you drink. They also contain gluten, which can be problematic to those with sensitivities.

HARD LIQUOR OR SPIRITS such as vodka, tequila, and rum are much higher in alcohol than both wine and beer, which is why they're often diluted with tonic water or fruit juice. Be especially careful of these because of the high alcohol content.

NOW YOU HAVE an idea of some of the best foods to pick while dining out. How do you put these ideas into practice? First, remember the Five Keys to Clean Eating:

1 There's more than one right way to eat.
2 The overwhelming majority of your diet should consist of natural, high-quality and whole foods.
3 Everyone would be better off if a larger proportion of their diet consisted of plants—mostly vegetables (in particular, leafy greens), and some nuts, seeds and fruits.
4 If you choose to eat animal products, consume only (a) high-quality and sustainably raised animals (ideally pasture-raised and grass-fed, but at least hormone- and antibiotic-free), and do so (b) in moderation—meaning smaller portions with less frequency.
5 To feel better immediately, reduce your intake of artificial, chemical-laden processed foods as well as sugar, caffeine and alcohol.

We want to make it easy for you to transition—and stick—to healthier dining, so here are several psychological and social tips for following what's outlined above.

MOTIVATION

This is the why: You've got to know why you're doing something to do it successfully. So, why are you changing your diet? We all want to be slimmer, trimmer, better looking. And those are OK reasons. But there are better reasons, like heightened energy, greater strength, fewer illnesses and clearer thinking. It helps to get excited about getting the most out of life and bringing enjoyment not only to yourself but also to other people—not to mention planet Earth— since our food choices have a major impact on the environment.

So, right now, take out a sheet of paper and write down why you want to eat healthier. Once you've written down your motivations, commit to them—that is, set a clear intention. It's a great launching pad for getting—and staying—motivated.

The other part of intention and motivation? Believing that, yes, you can do this. Don't simply hope you can succeed; know that you will.

AWARENESS

Awareness means (a) remembering your motivation (your why) and intention (your commitment); and (b) being aware of the various forces that might act against you. Admitting that challenges exist is a necessary step to moving beyond them. These challenges may include things like physical cravings and addictions, emotional attachments to food, cultural conditioning, advertising and a lack of education about healthy eating. Peer pressure is another biggie; you're going to need to keep your resolve if others try to coax you back to your old ways. Be aware that change can make others uncomfortable.

Awareness also means paying attention to how certain foods make you feel, physically and mentally. Keep a diet diary if that helps.

Begin to eliminate any foods or drinks that drain your energy, give you indigestion, make you irritable or create so much guilt when you consume them that you simply don't enjoy or digest them properly.

PATIENCE

Do you wish there was a magic formula for positive change? Actually, there is. Think of it as the magical trio: patience, perseverance and resilience. And yes, we know, these qualities aren't so simple.

In dietary terms, these words mean realizing that lasting improvements take time and application. At first you may need to be satisfied with eating healthier about half of the time, but once you do get to that 50/50 mark, you will have the momentum to go further, slowly, going from 60/40 to 70/30 and onward, until you may even hit 90/10. Don't be too extreme right away, though.

YOUR CHOICES AS AN INDIVIDUAL

Part of being human is having the ability to make conscious choices based on our intentions and what is best for us. Just start with the 50 percent rule and see what happens. En route, don't be discouraged by slip-ups. Notice them and move on. Try not to be too rigid with yourself or others. People who are hard on themselves tend to be judgmental of others. That's counterproductive. If your mission to eat better becomes a strict chore and strains your relationships, it will make you miserable and you will long for your old, comfortable ways. Remember, what works for your body may not necessarily work for someone else's; that's bio-individuality.

HOW TO EAT

STAY NOURISHED: Stay on top of cravings by beginning the day with a sustaining breakfast and a nutritious lunch. Make lunch your largest meal of the day, and when possible eat a fairly light dinner early—a large salad or vegetarian option, for instance—so you're not overeating close to bedtime. And keep hydrated all day by drinking water.

CHEW: It seems obvious, but you'd be surprised how many people don't, at least not properly. Thorough mastication helps your body digest nutrients better. To see just how little chewing we all do, try chewing 10 to 20 times per mouthful or until the food becomes liquid—not easy, right?

EAT SLOWLY: Pause between bites to savor the flavors and check in with your stomach to ask it "Are you full yet?" This will make your meal last longer and help to prevent the discomfort and weight gain associated with overeating.

DON'T OVEREAT: Eating slowly and chewing properly helps to prevent this, but note how much you order in the first place. Practice portion control. And realize that it's unnecessary to order an appetizer and dessert as well as an entrée. If you're still hungry after eating slowly, you can always order more. Have a light fruit snack before going out to eat; if you arrive at a restaurant starving, you're likely to overeat. And skip the bread at the beginning of the meal.

AVOID DISTRACTIONS: If you're not good at blocking out extraneous noise and distractions, you might want to eat in silence or alone occasionally. But given that most meals—especially in restaurants—are a fun, shared experience, try to dine with people who don't give you indigestion. Keep heated debates to a minimum so that you can chew and assimilate the food properly. Reading and television are also distracting.

DON'T EAT UNDER STRESS: Anxiety and anger shut down the digestive function as part of the "fight or flight" response. Eating under such circumstances can cause indigestion. At such times you will be tempted to go for comfort foods or to overeat to numb your feelings. If you do arrive stressed at a restaurant, take a few deep breaths and remember your intention.

PRACTICE GRATITUDE: Be thankful for your food and for all the people and forces that brought it to your table: the sun that shone down on it, the farmer who grew it and the waiter who delivered it. Taking a moment to give thanks will calm you and remind you of your connection to the whole. It will also enable you to feel grateful for real, healthy food and simple pleasures.

ENJOY: Whatever you choose to eat—even if you know it is not perfectly healthy—allow yourself to enjoy it. Guilt is a stressor that makes you and your digestive system unhappy.

EXPERIMENT: It's that bio-individuality thing again. Experiment with different dietary theories and foods so that over time you can discover what works best for you and your body. At the very least, eat a few meals each week with no animal products by ordering proteins such as beans. Whatever you do, eat your veggies!

SOCIAL SITUATIONS

Even with the best intentions you will occasionally end up at a restaurant that does not serve healthy food or with a group of diners who do not share your dietary goals.

What to do?

ORDER SIDES: Most restaurants have a selection of side dishes from which you can create a meal.

SPECIAL ORDER: An accommodating, creative chef will be happy to make something especially for you. Try requests like: "I know it's not on the menu, but could you put together a plate of vegetables and beans for me?" or "I'd like an extra-large version of your side salad as my entrée."

SKIP THE FREEBIES: Just because the bread is complimentary does

61

not mean that you have to eat it. Likewise, try to ignore those fortune cookies or mints that arrive with the bill.

ASK FOR SAUCE ON THE SIDE: If the salad dressings and sauces are not up to par, ask the server to bring them on the side so you can monitor how much you use.

ASK FOR SUBSTITUTIONS: Some restaurants charge for doing this, and some don't. In any case, it is worth asking for things like green veggies or even baked potatoes instead of french fries.

WHAT TO ASK
When the cooking is out of your control, it's hard to know exactly what you're about to consume and where it has come from. Here are some illuminating questions to ask your server.

How was this prepared?
Some establishments make meals from scratch, while others pre-make recipes in bulk and microwave them on demand, or plate veggies and fruits straight from the can. By asking your server how your dish has been prepared (Was it sautéed? Boiled? Steamed?) you can gather a bit more information for peace of mind.

Can I substitute?
Always see if you can swap for a more whole option. For example, see if you can get brown rice in place of white.

Where was this sourced from? Is it organic?
It may feel awkward at first, but getting into the habit of questioning your server about whether your chicken is organic or your hamburger is from a grass-fed source is an important way of ensuring you aren't consuming added hormones or antibiotics.

Want to know if your veggies have been sautéed in a low-quality oil? If your cake has been made with margarine? Your servers are meant to be a resource. Use them!

Routinely asking these questions is a great way to build your "food radar"—a muscle of sorts that will grow stronger with use. The more you check for the differences between whole and unwholesome, high-quality and run-of-the-mill, real and processed, the more automatic eating real, whole and high-quality foods will become.

Hopefully you now have enough inspiration, motivation and information to put the Five Keys to Clean Eating into action. It's time to start enjoying your food more than ever while getting healthier at the same time. You can have your naturally sweetened dessert and eat it, too!

So now let's get to the best part (we have a feeling you may have taken a peek already) and check out the restaurants.

THE CLEAN PLATES 100 NYC

Clean Meats
The majority of meats served are, at a minimum, antibiotic- and hormone-free

Clean Fish
The majority of seafood served is from sustainable fisheries

Vegetarian-Friendly
A vegetarian can happily dine here

Clean Desserts
Emphasis on organic ingredients and natural sweeteners

Gluten-Free-Friendly
Those with gluten sensitivities can happily dine here

Grab-and-Go
Online ordering available for pick-up and/or fast food options

Delivers

$15 and Under
Meal for one

$15–$30

$30–$60

$60 and Up

THE TOP FIVES

A round-up of our top picks for specific dietary wants and needs.

BRUNCH

FLEXITARIAN

*(Accommodates vegetarians, meat-eaters
and those with gluten sensitivities)*

GLUTEN-FREE

PALEO-FRIENDLY

VEGETARIAN/VEGAN

SPECIAL OCCASION

ABC KITCHEN

35 E. 18th St.
212-475-5829

abckitchennyc.com
@ABCKitchen

ABC COCINA

38 E. 19th St.
212-677-2233

abccocinanyc.com
@ABCCocina

Cuisine: American
(Contemporary), Latin
American (ABC Cocina)

Neighborhood:
Union Square

Meals Served:
Brunch, Lunch, Dinner

Gorgeous housewares shopping with a side of upscale, sustainable dining? Oh yes, please. Chef Jean-Georges Vongerichten set up shop in the eco-minded furnishings store ABC Carpet and Home in 2010, and the beautiful crowds have been packing the white-washed floors ever since.

Come here to peruse racks of rumpled-just-so organic linens, then retire to the restaurant for dishes such as pretzel-dusted calamari, roasted portobello and celery leaves, all plated on antique dishes.

The kitchen crafts a menu with brilliant offerings that elevate vegetables to their highest calling. Carrots are caramelized and happily paired with buttery avocados, crunchy seeds, sour cream and citrus in a starter salad. Whole-wheat pizzas and a rotating selection of toasts, like the Peekytoe crab with fresh lemon aioli, are particular standouts.

Next door at the equally stylish ABC Cocina, the local game stays the same but the influence is a global riot of Spanish and Latin flavors. Start with the guacamole studded with sunflower seeds and English peas and let the wave of small plates carry you from there.

CLEAN BITES

- Menu is free of pesticides, synthetic fertilizers, insecticides, antibiotics, hormones and GMO foods.

Cuisine:
Italian

Neighborhood:
Park Slope

Meals Served:
Brunch, Lunch, Dinner

AL DI LA TRATTORIA

248 5th Ave.

718-783-4565

aldilatrattoria.com

@aldilabrooklyn

If you like Italian food, you may come to believe that Al di la is the best restaurant in Brooklyn.

It is peaceful here even when it is packed, which is pretty much always.

It truly does not matter what you order; it is all delicious. Eat house-made pasta, eat salads. Eat the hanger steak "tagliata," in which the fatty cut is made delicate by slicing thinly and cooking to a medium-rare. Definitely eat the daily fish, usually grilled simply and served with a vegetable. You won't be able to stop eating the farro salad with mint and spring onions. Do not miss the famous braised rabbit with black olives and polenta.

Al di la does not take reservations. It takes your name and phone number, tells you your wait time, and sends you to its wine bar around the corner. Just wait and sip—it will be worth it.

CLEAN BITES

- Al di la holds a Snail of Approval from Slow Food NYC.
- Don't despair the wait times; a compensatory glass of prosecco is often offered when the wait drags on longer than promised.

ALMANAC

28 7th Ave.
212-255-1795

almanacnyc.com
@Almanacnyc

Cuisine:
American

Neighborhood:
West Village

Meals Served:
Dinner

$$$$

Chef Galen Zamarra—also of Mas (farmhouse)—is not just into seasonality, he's a proponent of micro-seasons. Zamarra believes that each part of the season (for instance, early fall, mid fall and late fall) has its own distinctive bounty, rhythm and growing cycle nuance.

Everything at this West Village fine-dining spot reflects those beliefs. For example, Zamarra juices his squash at the beginning of its harvest and roasts it at the end, because the squash's moisture changes throughout the season. Nose-to-tail here doesn't just refer to eliminating waste and using the whole animal, but also to the fish and vegetables he sources—no part gets left behind.

Many flavors are unexpected. Zamarra uses the wintry taste of pine in a dish of wild steelhead trout smoked with pine and juniper and a dish of celery root carpaccio draped with shaved matsutake mushrooms, pine aioli and a smoked pine vinegar.

Experience his hyper-seasonal vision with a three-course menu for $75, five-courses for $95, or eight for $145. Wine pairings are also available for each tasting menu.

CLEAN BITES

- Miss the formality of yesteryear? This is your spot: Overhead circular iron chandeliers lend intimate light and the tables have honest-to-goodness linen tablecloths.
- Almanac offers a semi-private dining room that can accommodate up to 34 people. It is adorned with reclaimed and weathered pine from Massachusetts, gold-flecked cork and antique mirrors.

Cuisine:
Mediterranean,
Seafood

Neighborhood:
Upper East Side

Meals Served:
Brunch, Lunch, Dinner

AMALI

115 E. 60th St.
212-339-8363

amalinyc.com
@amalinyc

Midtown doesn't get closer to the Mediterranean than the dining room of Amali.

In an age when many chefs scour the globe for boast-worthy ingredients, Amali's Rachel Goulet prefers to prepare Greek-inspired food from a nearly all-local supply of ingredients, including seafood, produce and grass-fed meat. The result is a menu that is as fresh and flavorful as if it had been prepared on the beach in Mykonos.

Start the meal with baby lettuces or a plate of gently charred octopus. Seafood, sourced from local fishermen, could include line-caught grilled dorade or pan seared salmon. In classic Greek tradition, lamb is a staple on the menu, although the cut changes frequently, depending on availability.

For dessert? Try the sparkling rosé float with strawberry rhubarb sorbet or the chocolate chip cookies made with chickpea flour. Pair it all with a biodynamic or natural wine from the 400-bottle list and enjoy Amali's local Odyssey.

CLEAN BITES

- Must try: The signature dorade is line-caught off Montauk and so fresh that it requires nothing more than a delicate swab of olive oil and lemon with a bit of thyme.
- The upstairs communal dining and private event space, Sopra, serves an ever-changing tasting menu of the very best seasonal finds.
- The restaurant staff educates schoolchildren about local, sustainable eating.

APPLEWOOD

501 11th St.
718-788-1810

applewoodny.com
@applewoodny

Cuisine:
American
(Contemporary)

Neighborhood:
Park Slope

Meals Served:
Brunch, Dinner

At Applewood, flavors encourage curiosity, prompt questions and often steal your focus from your date.

After a day in the chaotic city, who wouldn't be drawn to the country-style chairs, sprigs of lavender on the table and warm lighting?

The Sheas, the power couple who own and run the restaurant, are devoted to supporting local farmers and serving sustainable seafood and hormone-free meats and poultry.

Knowledgeable servers are happy to answer questions. Wondering what gives white bean puree on whole-wheat bread such a pleasant heat? A waiter will happily inform you that it is pickled chilies that infuse complexity into the humble spread.

The seafood here is particularly good: Taste the Sheas' devotion in Atlantic mahi mahi with crisp pea shoots or the expertly pan roasted Atlantic striped bass is served crispy skin-side up over toasted wheatberries, grilled onions and sweet roasted carrot puree.

CLEAN BITES

- Applewood's owners travel back and forth from their upstate farm bringing produce and animals to the restaurant and compostable materials back to the farm.
- Warm up! There is a fireplace crackling here during winter, as if the rest of the country charm wasn't enough to seduce diners.

Cuisine:
Italian

Neighborhood: Soho,
Williamsburg

Meals Served:
Brunch, Lunch, Dinner

AURORA

510 Broome St.
212-334-9020

aurorasoho.com
@AuroraSoho

70 Grand St.
718-388-5100

aurorabk.com
@AURORAbk

When you dine at a trattoria on the southern Italian coast there are romances you can expect: smells of ocean water in the air and the click-click-click of heels navigating cobblestoned streets.

At Aurora, somehow, the food conveys this.

Different seasons bring different incarnations of a straightforward southern Italian menu: antipasti (salads, carpaccio, flatbread), primi (pastas with various seasonal vegetables) and secondi (fish of the day, roasted half-chicken, steak, veal loin).

Portions are generous—an heirloom tomato salad with burrata, basil and bread crumbs was almost too big to finish, but we did, because not much is better than an heirloom tomato with olive oil and sea salt in the middle of August. The fish of the day, a whole Mediterranean sea bass, was flaky, fresh and an enormous portion for one person; plus, it was abundantly outfitted with steamed broccoli rabe and roasted sunchokes.

You almost won't miss that Amalfi sunset.

CLEAN BITES

- The outdoor garden at their Brooklyn location is particularly quaint.
- No need to ask: All the pasta, bread and desserts are made on the premises.
- There is a good selection of organic and biodynamic wines here.

BACK FORTY WEST

70 Prince St.
212-219-8570

backfortynyc.com
@BackFortyWest

Cuisine:
American
(Contemporary)

Neighborhood: Soho

Meals Served:
Brunch, Lunch, Dinner

Back Forty West is run by Chef Peter Hoffman, whose locavore ways inspire the comforting farm-to-table cuisine that is put forth. Walls lined with mismatched plates, crumbling exposed brick, wood panels and subtle lighting somehow translate into a chic rustic ambiance.

Start off your experience reaching across the table, bumping elbows and celebrating good food with shared plates; we love the beet ricotta mint crostinis and mezze plate with vegetable crudité.

The smoky char of grilled carp is balanced with a sweet fig and walnut anchoiade that excels, as does the grass-fed steak with earthy mushrooms and herbs. Your classic caesar salad wishes it was always as good as a grilled kale version that comes with chili-marinated anchovies and country bread standing in for croutons. One item you might have a hard time splitting: the justly famous grass-fed burger.

CLEAN BITES

- Keep your eyes peeled for produce-pedaling chef Peter Hoffman at the Greenmarket.
- Join the mailing list to stay informed of seasonal events like summer crab boils and fried chicken dinners.
- On weekends, grab coffee and pastries to-go and stroll through the Soho streets!

BAREBURGER

Multiple locations

bareburger.com
@Bareburger

What started as one burger joint serving up tasty, organic burgers and fries in Astoria, Queens, has grown into 23 (and counting) lively locations across the tri-state area.

The menu abounds with choice, so all your friends, whether gluten-free, vegetarian or carnivorous, will find something to enjoy. First, pick from a panoply of burger styles, including the SoCal, with sharp cheddar and guacamole, or the Farmstead with sweet potato and cauliflower hummus. Then match your style with one of the many proteins (including unique offerings like a quinoa patty, bison, elk and wild boar) and also from a slew of bun options (including forgoing one altogether for a collard greens wrap). Little touches like organic condiments, vegan cheese, agave nectar for sweetening, multiple dipping sauces and a kids' menu show that Bareburger is eager to please.

Take caution: It is easy to overindulge—remember, an organic milkshake is still a milkshake. Nevertheless, if you are going for the burger-fries-and-shake trinity, it may as well be at a luscious, organic, eco-conscious restaurant that has low-energy toilets and walls lined with repurposed wood.

CLEAN BITES

- Counting calories? Bareburger offers a fun Interactive Nutrition Menu online.
- Even the condiments are organic! No high fructose corn syrup here.

BELL BOOK & CANDLE

141 W. 10th St.

212-414-2355

bbandcnyc.com

@johnmooney5

Cuisine:
American
(Contemporary)

Neighborhood:
Greenwich Village

Meals Served:
Brunch, Dinner

The intriguing atmosphere inside Bell Book & Candle, an eatery nearly hidden beneath West 10th Street, makes it easy to forget what's overhead: an equally beguiling rooftop aeroponic garden. Numerous vegetables and herbs are grown on-site for use in the restaurant, which is the cherry on top of an impressively sustainable operation. Complimentary sparkling and still filtered water is bottled on-site, gobs of local cheeses are available, and fruit-centric cocktails have unexpected additions such as roof top mint or guajillo chili salt.

Don't miss a salad from the "Living Leaf" section of the menu, like the Rooftop Mixed Greens, which uses the couldn't-be-more-local produce. Buttery bibb lettuce, subtly spicy varieties of arugula and bits of frisée are finished with crisp cucumbers, firm grape tomatoes and a delicately sweet Thousand Island dressing.

Although intent on making the most of seasonal produce, the restaurant doesn't hold back on proteins: Think delightfully juicy grilled lamb chops slicked with a lemon, oregano and olive oil glaze and grilled hanger steak with onion marmalade.

CLEAN BITES

- If you are curious to learn more about the restaurant's vertical rooftop garden system, visit towergarden.com.
- The restaurant encompasses many spaces, each with its own feel. When making a reservation, pick from the main dining room with a view of the kitchen or the back dining room with tufted blue booths, or grab a seat in the sexy bar area.

Cuisine:
Japanese, Vegetarian/
Vegan

Meals Served:
Lunch, Dinner

BEYOND SUSHI

Multiple locations

beyondsushinyc.com
@BeyondSushi

Imagine sushi without fish: delicious rolls made of fresh vegetables, fruits and rice, and 100% vegan. Guy Vaknin, a former contestant on Gordon Ramsey's "Hell's Kitchen," slings these innovative rolls at three locations.

Each made-to-order roll is a carefully constructed whorl of colorful vegetables, fruits, and nutritious black or six-grain rice. We're particularly wild about the Spicy Mang, in which a rainbow of ripe avocado, mango and crisp cucumber strips are rolled in a perfect rectangle of rice. A spicy toasted cayenne dressing is then draped over the entire roll.

All locations are as compact as the rolls themselves, so take your sushi and custom sauces in innovative plastic tubes, that look like they came straight out of a chemistry lab, to-go.

If sushi rolls aren't your game, gluten-free rice paper wraps, rice-bed salads, soups, naturally sweetened desserts and fresh juices are also available.

CLEAN BITES

- Make sure to inquire about the extra-creative Roll of the Month and Piece of the Month specials.
- The kitchen only uses olive oil.

BLACK TREE SANDWICH SHOP

131 Orchard St.   blacktreenyc.com
212-533-4684   @BlackTreeNYC

$$

Cuisine:
American (Casual)

Neighborhood:
Lower East Side

Meals Served:
Brunch, Lunch,
Dinner

The weekly menu at Black Tree goes whole hog. It also goes whole rabbit, cow, lamb and duck. This is because the tiny Lower East Side restaurant and sandwich shop brings in one whole animal at a time, creating an entire menu section around its various cuts.

The resulting four-to-six-dish lineup is one of the most creative concepts in town. Whole grass-fed lamb could appear on the menu as ribs, a leg-of-lamb sandwich, seared chops and offal tacos. Heritage pig butchered in-house could become a pan-fried pâté banh mi, a hulking porterhouse, pulled pork with house pickles, and a steaming bowl of tonkotsu ramen with a loin chop.

The owners source everything from within a 300-mile radius, ensuring fresh, seasonal ingredients for every dish, including several excellent vegetarian dishes, like a seasonal portobello mushroom sandwich with ricotta cheese.

Whether or not you dine whole hog, Black Tree excels.

CLEAN BITES

- Must try: the signature pig sandwich—showcasing pork belly braised in local IPA—changes its ingredients and name with the seasons. We recommend a visit for each iteration.
- The restaurant was built using reclaimed wood and salvaged components.

Cuisine:
American
(Contemporary)

Neighborhood:
West Village

Meals Served:
Brunch, Lunch, Dinner

BLENHEIM

283 W. 12th St.
212-243-7073

blenheimhill.com
@BlenheimNYC

$$$

Blenheim takes terroir to a whole new level: Every dish on its menu trumpets the bounty of one parcel of land upstate, sourcing almost entirely from its eponymous 150-acre farm in the Catskills with a menu that changes daily based on the harvest.

Unsurprisingly, the ingredients are exceptional. The farm raises free-roaming heritage livestock sheep, cattle, pigs and chickens. The lettuce, flowers and herbs thrive year-round in an astounding hydroponic greenhouse.

Get a first taste of the results in the Blenheim salad, which tosses together nine lettuces from the farm with a citrus vinaigrette. Also from the farm: Nature's Bounty, a daily selection of raw, cooked and pickled vegetables and Blenheim's shortrib that arrives with eggplant, cherry tomato with pasilla chili.

On beautiful nights, the restaurant opens up sidewalk seating. It may not be a meal outdoors on a farm, but it's as close as Manhattan can get.

CLEAN BITES

- All of the restaurant's produce comes from Blenheim Hill, a farm in the Catskills owned by the restaurateurs.
- Must try: the pork. The menu changes daily based on what's available at the farm, but pork is a winning bet any time it appears, since the farm's pigs are heritage breeds that forage year-round.
- Each plate is a work of art. Chef Mazen Mustafa masterfully incorporates herbs, greens and edible blossoms to create edible palettes.

BLOSSOM

Multiple locations

blossomnyc.com
@BlossomVegan

Cuisine:
Vegetarian/Vegan

Meals Served:
Brunch, Lunch, Dinner

Vegan and raw-food restaurants sometimes have a formal, slightly sterile air that seems to shout: "Healthy food is on the premises!" Not so at any member of the Blossom family.

Blossom is a fine way to introduce naysayers to gourmet vegan cuisine at its finest. Several different regions of the world see a brief spin in the menu limelight at the various locations. The American South makes a cameo in a crisp cake of potatoes and black-eyed peas in a puddle of spicy chipotle aioli. An Italian tip of the hat comes via delicate ravioli floating in cashew cream flecked with sage and cremini mushrooms. Of the naturally sweetened desserts occasionally on offer, we loved a silky lavender tartlet sprinkled with über-fresh blueberries.

A sister spot, Blossom Du Jour, is perfect when you are in need of 100% vegan food fast. Stop in for sandwiches, wraps and salads, like the Karmic Kale Salad with tahini dressing, or a cold-pressed juice.

CLEAN BITES

- Blossom's baked goods are also available at Whole Foods (Chelsea and Union Square locations).
- Check out their website for a virtual tour of their Chelsea location.

Cuisine:
American
(Contemporary)

Neighborhood:
Greenwich Village

Meals Served:
Dinner

BLUE HILL

75 Washington Pl.
212-539-1776

bluehillfarm.com
@bluehillfarm

$$$$

Most people name-drop the executive chef of Blue Hill with the same friendly familiarity as that of their local barista or SnapChat friend, but we are sure not everyone is as acquainted with Dan Barber as they would like to be. Whether he is being honored by the president or receiving a James Beard award, Chef Barber keeps himself humble and his conversations intellectual. The chef is as in tune with his food as he is with agriculture, which translates into properly sourced, perfectly prepared, professionally playful plates.

At Blue Hill, guests can choose from the daily menu or opt for the Farmer's Feast, a five-course tasting inspired by the week's harvest. The space is elegant and serene, with cushy red chairs and banquettes lining the walls, and the staff is charming—ideal conditions for traipsing through a menu chock-full of local, seasonal, organic ingredients. All dairy comes straight from Barber's farm upstate, the locale of his other wonderful eatery, Blue Hill at Stone Barns.

If you imbibe, this is the place to do it. The wine list is packed with producers who respect artisanal techniques and practice organic and biodynamic winemaking.

CLEAN BITES

- Check out the Stone Barns Center for Food and Agriculture, just 30 miles north of NYC—a working, four-season farm and education center Blue Hill partners with.
- The restaurant is hidden, three steps below street level, just off Washington Square Park. Keep your eyes peeled: It often takes first-timers two passes to find it.

BRUSHSTROKE

30 Hudson St.
212-791-3771

davidbouley.com
@davidbouley

Cuisine:
Japanese

Neighborhood:
Tribeca

Meals Served:
Lunch, Dinner

Executive chef and New York institution David Bouley has partnered with the Tsuji Culinary Institute of Osaka to prepare traditional Japanese dishes with just a hint of fusion. The restaurant's main room has the lovely, spare feel of a Buddhist shrine in which every detail is just so, from the large, rice paper–lined windows to the rough, honey-colored wooden walls.

Meals are prepared by instructors from Tsuji and overseen by chef Isao Yamada, and are the result of thousands of hours of collaborative research. Traditionally, a kaiseki menu, which originated in the imperial courts of Kyoto, comprises a series of small plates artfully arranged with an eye to color and form and with a strong emphasis on seasonal flavors. Brushstroke offers two such tasting menus per night, but those looking for a lighter meal will be well satisfied with the equally meticulous a la carte offerings, which arrive on the table like tiny, edible still-life paintings. All the meats at Brushstroke are certified organic, and all tofu is sourced from Japan.

CLEAN BITES

- Must try: chawan-mushi, a traditional egg custard served in a teacup made unique with golden crab and truffle mushrooms.
- The restaurant offers a vegetarian tasting menu.

BUBBY'S

73 Gansevoort St.
212-206-6200

bubbys.com
@bubbys

120 Hudson St.
212-219-0666

$$

This restaurant may have you re-evaluating your preconceived notion of the Yiddish term "bubby."

The ardently American menu lists "things we do to make good food for you" which includes everything from frying in organic, non-GMO, expeller-pressed canola oil to sourcing fish, flour, meat and milk from New York State sources.

Barbecue, which is slow-smoked on the premises using local hogs and wood, is the specialty here. The basin-size barbecue sampler includes chile-crusted ribs, smoked sausage and root beer glazed smoked chicken, and comes with two sides (we are fans of the broccoli and baked fava beans).

Bubby's grinds meat daily for its mammoth grass-fed burger which emerges from the kitchen a ruddy medium-rare, its juices forming a beefy puddle for the crisp fries and a homemade dill pickle on the side. To even things out, order a seasonal vegetable plate loaded with farmers-market greens or a side of spinach sautéed with ample amounts of garlic.

CLEAN BITES

- Bubby's ships their homemade pies to anywhere within the United States.
- Bubby's employs a forager who works with local farmers, visits local markets and forages wild plants. Visit their website to learn more about their purveyors.

THE BUTCHER'S DAUGHTER

19 Kenmare St. thebutchersdaughter.com
212-219-3434 @TBDjuicebarcafe

Cuisine:
Vegetarian/Vegan

Neighborhood:
Nolita

Meals Served:
Breakfast, Brunch,
Lunch, Dinner

The Butcher's Daughter treats fruits and vegetables as a butcher would meat: The cooks here chop, fillet and carve fresh produce into vegetarian dishes and press them into pretty juices.

Actually, everything here is attractive—from the white-painted brick and the corner windows to a watermelon ricotta salad with toasted sunflower seeds and date vinaigrette.

The beautiful scene is no surprise since Heather Tierney, who is also behind Apothéke and Pulqueria, is the driving force behind the space.

Some things on the menu, like the kale salad with avocado, green apples and smoked sea salt, are constants, but the 100% vegetarian and non-dairy menu frequently changes. There are always plenty of vegan and gluten-free options, and the kitchen is more than understanding about dietary restrictions.

Dinner is more substantial, with white-bean fennel sausage and a zucchini and carrot pasta topped with black bean-tomato Bolognese.

With all-day dining, feel free to stop in whenever the mood strikes.

CLEAN BITES

- Stop in next door at The Butcher's Daughter Market for provisions and juices like the Hangover Killer—young Thai coconut, pineapple, yuzu, chili, evening primrose oil and cilantro.
- The restaurant works with its own local-produce forager—check out what produce is being highlighted each month on the website's produce calendar.
- The Butcher's Daughter offers one-, three- and five-day juice and raw food cleanses.

Cuisine:
American

Neighborhood:
Greenwich Village

Meals Served:
Brunch, Lunch, Dinner

CAFÉ CLOVER

10 Downing St.

cafeclovernyc.com

212-675-4350

@cafeclovernyc

Since you can't have a nutritionist follow you around everywhere you go, Café Clover has staffed one for you.

Here, Peak Performance nutritionist Mike Roussell and chef David Standridge team up to review every dish coming out of Standridge's kitchen.

Instead of a basket of bread, meals start with homemade flaxseed, sesame and pumpkin seed crackers. A finely shredded kale salad (one of the five rotating market salads that top the menu) is enlivened with bursts of blood orange slices and crunchy watermelon radishes.

Dishes like risotto look like the picture of indulgence, but its luxuriousness is due to slowly cooking lentils in vegetable stock and then pureeing them with just the slightest touch of organic cream.

The menu is full of good-for-you ingredients (locally sourced and organic whenever possible) without losing any of the fun, flavor and excitement of dining out at a truly pretty Greenwich Village dinner and drinks spot.

CLEAN BITES

- Café Clover is a hive for learning about new techniques (cauliflower steak) and new ingredients (ivory lentils) to transfer to the home kitchen.
- The 70-seat dining room is broken into intimate sections with soft blue banquettes.

CANDLE 79

154 E. 79th St.
212-537-7179

candle79.com
@candle79

Cuisine:
Vegetarian/Vegan

Neighborhoods: Upper
East Side, Multiple
locations (Candle Cafe)

Meals Served:
Brunch, Lunch, Dinner

CANDLE CAFE

Multiple locations

candlecafe.com

The twin Candle Cafes are old-school in the best way. The original East Side location has been a vegan hot spot since 1994. The square wooden tables and casual vibe make this a take-your-mom-to-lunch-and-show-her-vegan-food-is-tasty sort of place.

Those stopping in for a drink and a snack should indulge in a satisfying Mezza Plate including buttery-tasting hummus and lemon-date chutney for the zataar, or a hearty, tasty "Aztec" salad topped with sticks of grilled tempeh and punched up with corn, beans and a mélange of greens.

If nothing else, stop in for a slice of chocolate mousse pie. The chocolate treat is absolutely decadent; tofu and coconut oil are whipped into a silky mousse that's decidedly un-tofulike, with a crumbly, chocolatey spelt crust that tastes nothing like spelt.

Candle 79 is a posh elder sister; it offers a greatest-hits list of all-organic, vegan fare. The fancier, split-level spot is a romantic go-to with a wine list featuring several biodynamic options.

CLEAN BITES

- Candle Cafe was funded by money won in a Take 5 lottery on a Friday the 13th!
- If you want to take Candle Cafe home, try the restaurant's line of foods available at Whole Foods.

85

Cuisine:
Raw, Vegetarian/Vegan

Neighborhood:
East Village

Meals Served:
Brunch, Lunch, Dinner

CARAVAN OF DREAMS

405 E. 6th St.

caravanofdreams.net

212-254-1613

@caravanofdreams

Since 1991, this assertively hippie-ish restaurant has offered a kaleidoscopic array of vegan, kosher and raw foods.

Smoothie-cravers should definitely put this on their map; we count a couple dozen fresh juices and shakes, along with booze like sangria and several organic wines. Chill waiters seem unconcerned if you hang out for an hour or two over a beverage and a plate of "live" raw nachos: flaxseed chips with super-smooth guacamole, bright pico de gallo and almond sour cream.

We love the sampler tapas platter with hummus, pesto, guacamole, smoked eggplant spread and herbed cashew kefir. On the health front, the eatery wins points for abundant organic options, including more than a dozen salads and the fact that sandwiches are available on sprouted whole-grain bread. There are plenty of gluten-free choices like the breakfast burrito stuffed with potatoes, kale, guacamole, smoked tofu and chile de árbol.

For those seeking a meatless meal, this spot truly is a caravan of dreams.

CLEAN BITES

- The restaurant features live music every night and during weekend brunch.
- Caravan of Dreams is under the supervision of the Orthodox Kashruth Supervision Services and everything is kosher, except on Passover.
- Online ordering is available.

CHARLIE BIRD

5 King St.
212-235-7133

charliebirdnyc.com
@CharlieBirdNYC

Cuisine:
Italian

Neighborhood:
Soho

Meals Served:
Lunch, Dinner

The folks at Charlie Bird are passionate about wine, and boy does it show.

Sommelier Robert Bohr might be a heavyweight in the wine world, but wining and dining here is completely unstuffy, verging on happily raucous some nights. The gorgeously thin wine glasses are reason enough to order a glass, but the staff's enthusiasm and knowledge of the wine list (many by-the-glass options are available) makes it practically obligatory.

Once you've picked what you are drinking, move on to the Italian-inspired menu with its silken pastas and raw fish preparations. Charlie Bird boasts that its menu comes from "New York's farmers markets, Long Island fishing boats, country fields and the wounderous meanderings of spirited travelers with passionate palates," brought to life with beef carpaccio, pine nuts and fennel; farro salad , pistachios and roasted peas; and strawberry and burrata, which hit the table like a welcome storm. Along with larger plates of sea bream and roasted chicken, there are always plentiful vegetable options to pick from: crispy squash blossoms highlighted with ricotta, baby eggplant streaked with garlic and vinegar and caramelized cauliflower sprinkled with hazelnuts—just to get you salivating.

CLEAN BITES

- If you over-imbibed the night before, you can order juices like the Kidney Punch (orange, turmeric, beet and ginger) at lunch.
- All the meats are certified organic.

Cuisine:
Mexican

Meals Served:
Lunch, Dinner

CHIPOTLE

Multiple locations

chipotle.com
@ChipotleTweets

With the tagline "Farm-to-Face," Chipotle takes the farm-to-table concept, wraps it in a tortilla, and gets it to your mouth with impressive speed and flavor.

The customizable burritos and tacos are built from quality ingredients that reflect the chain's dedication to "food with integrity"—that is, produce and proteins raised with respect for the animals, the environment and the farmers.

Join the assembly-line-style queue and be ready to declare your choice of protein (no dawdling!): either braised carnitas or barbacoa, or adobo-marinated-and-grilled chicken or steak. (Vegetarians can select grilled red onions and green bell peppers.) Top it with cilantro-lime rice and pinto or black beans, and calibrate the addition of super-fresh guacamole (their reknowned recipe is available on their website), cheese, sour cream and/or chili corn salsa to your liking.

As the burritos are humongous, try building your own salad or burrito bowl.

CLEAN BITES

- Chipotle is the first national restaurant chain to cook with only non-GMO ingredients. Or as they say, they are "GMover it."
- Most of the dairy products come from pasture-raised cows.
- The chain created its own Food With Integrity program to work with smaller, family-owned farms and ensure the quality of its produce, animal products and beans.

CITY BAKERY

3 W. 18th St.
212-366-1414

thecitybakery.com
@citybakery

Cuisine:
American (Casual)

Neighborhood:
Union Square

Meals Served:
Breakfast, Lunch

Many of us are lured through the inviting doors of City Bakery and—not seeing the forest for the trees—halt like 5-year-olds in front of the bubbling vats of hot chocolate.

Although the shop's thick cocoa is famous for a reason, be sure to sample the often-excellent, always local and mostly organic savory fare. Eco-friendly paper boxes can be filled with a myriad of eats to hustle over to one of several tiny tables in the split-level space. Hot and cold buffets feature fare that utterly defeats salad-bar stereotypes, including tuscan kale with pressed fennel juice and tofu baked with matcha tea, ginger and lime.

Leave it to owner Maury Rubin (who also hybridized a pretzel and croissant into the spot's iconic pretzel-croissant) to also offer distinct juices. We are wild about a foamy blend of cucumber, kale, spinach, orange and extra-virgin olive oil and a distinctive concoction of peanut butter and celery.

CLEAN BITES

- Must try: the hemp milk seeded scone.
- Check out Birdbath (p. 167), City Bakery's eco-friendly, sister establishment that serves baked goods with organic ingredients to-go (multiple locations). Arrive by bike and receive a discount.
- Keep an eye on City Bakery during February when it serves a different flavor of hot chocolate every day of the month as part of its Hot Chocolate Festival. (We all deserve a little treat once in a while.)

Cuisine:
American
(Contemporary)

Neighborhood:
Chelsea

Meals Served:
Brunch, Lunch, Dinner

COLICCHIO & SONS

85 10th Ave.
212-400-6699

craftrestaurantsinc.com
@Colicchio_Sons

If you are lucky and he's not critiquing Top Chef, you might catch celebrity chef Tom Colicchio manning the kitchen here, chef whites and all.

Oddly situated on a desolate street corner across from a gas station, Colicchio & Sons is Colicchio's reinvention of Craftsteak, a high-end steakhouse. The beauty of the space hasn't changed much (and neither has the slinky service) but the concept has—it's a bit more local and a tad more focused.

The vegetables and proteins here are carefully sourced from smaller farms that Colicchio has been working with for years, and the menu, which leans on Spanish and Indian flavors, is rooted in fine French technique and American comfort. In accordance with the market-driven movement, the menu changes often, so there are always gems to be discovered. Snacking on sheep's milk yogurt draped over summer melons under a glass fortress of the finest vintages at Colicchio & Sons while watching the top chef at work is an easy way to celebrate both locavorism and fine dining.

CLEAN BITES

- After a walk on the High Line or a long day at work check out the Tap Room, Colicchio & Sons more casual front room.
- Tom Colicchio is an ardent philanthropist and loves to give back to the community. Look out for special events that he and his team of restaurants put on throughout the year with groups such as Alex's Lemonade Stand and City Harvest.

COMMUNITY FOOD AND JUICE

2893 Broadway
212-665-2800

communityrestaurant.com

Cuisine:
American
(Contemporary)

Neighborhood:
Morningside Heights

Meals Served:
Breakfast, Brunch,
Lunch, Dinner

The fact that the proprietors of longtime downtown favorite Clinton Street Baking Company are still succeeding at comfort fare—even across town, in Morningside Heights—will come as no surprise to those who wait in long lines for their fare.

Health-friendly options abound here, starting with the beverages: Water is filtered, and there are a dozen organic or sustainable vino options. Vegetables prance happily across the menu, from a local zucchini-scallion pancake to a jewel-hued tender "bowl of beets" married to sweet goat cheese.

Among ample vegetarian options is the rice bowl—a simple mix of brown rice, prettily julienned carrots and cukes, bean sprouts and bright bits of cilantro and mint, with a sesame-lime dressing to tie everything together.

You can even end this meal feeling good: The eatery is certified by the Green Restaurant Association for its environmentally sound practices, from composting to energy-efficient kitchen equipment.

CLEAN BITES

- Check out the restaurant's website for a list of vendors.
- There are many gluten-free dessert options, as well as organic ice creams.
- Community employs a rigorous recycling and composting program.

Cuisine:
American
(Contemporary)

Neighborhood:
Chelsea

Meals Served:
Breakfast, Brunch,
Lunch, Dinner

COOKSHOP

156 10th Ave.
212-924-4440

cookshopny.com
@CookshopNY

Looking at art while gallivanting around Chelsea is hunger-inducing, so thank goodness for places like Cookshop, where you can enjoy a delicious meal in a space that feels like you haven't left the gallery.

Husband-wife team Victoria Freeman and Marc Meyer (see Hundred Acres [p. 116] and Vic's [p. 163]) pride themselves on sourcing locally, and it shows. For one, a giant chalkboard in the back of the restaurant features a diagram of a cow's edible parts. Try out the Mixed Grill, composed of lamb chop, hanger steak and pork tenderloin that sits atop yellow rice with sweet Medjool dates and almonds. This is an entree for the very hungry.

The tangy mix of peaches, vine beans, cucumber, red onion and goat milk feta topped with harissa vinaigrette combine to form a light, but filling summer salad and a vegetarian favorite.

Sea salt is on every table, so one can sprinkle a few crystals on anything lacking. Happily, at Cookshop, not much is, including the people-watching.

CLEAN BITES

- Transparency rules—just check the restaurant's website for a list of farms it gives its gratitude to.
- Cookshop supports multiple charities working to fight poverty and food injustice as well as improve our educational systems.
- There are raw milk cheeses on offer.

COUNTY

34 E. 20th St.
212-677-7771

countynyc.com
@Countynyc

$$$

Cuisine:
American
(Contemporary)

Neighborhood:
Flatiron

Meals Served:
Brunch, Lunch, Dinner

Walk off Union Square and let the whitewashed, reclaimed-barn walls and shelves lined with tin flower pots and homemade preserves transport you to a country farm stand awash in seasonal bounty. If it weren't for the very urban clientele—graphic designers packing into the bar area for post-work cocktails, new couples out on promising third dates—you'd be forgiven for imagining yourself on a romantic weekend getaway far from the city limits.

When County says farm-to-table, it means it literally: Executive chef Jan Feshan, formerly of ABC Kitchen (p. 67), sources his vegetables from the Union Square Greenmarket, just three blocks away. The eclectic menu continues the local-seasonal theme with fresh-from-the-garden offerings like shrimp salad with radish and chilled corn soup.

CLEAN BITES

- Must try for brunch: peanut butter and jelly french toast, and for dinner: roasted branzino with golden squash, zucchini and nasturtium vinaigrette.
- Feshan inherited the family culinary gene from his father, who once owned a five-story, 3,000-person catering business in Tehran. At age 11, he blustered his way into the kitchen and demanded to help peel eggplants. The rest is history.

Cuisine:
American (Traditional)

Neighborhood:
Flatiron

Meals Served:
Dinner

CRAFT

43 E. 19th St.
212-780-0880

craftrestaurantsinc.com
@Craft_NewYork

Despite the celeb-chef factor (at the helm is Top Chef judge Tom Colicchio) and the heavy-hitting clientele, there are few theatrics on the plate at Craft. The kitchen embraces elegant understatement in its approach to seasonal, contemporary, rich American cooking.

The menu—where items are often described in no more than one or two words—is minimalist. You definitely need to consult your knowledgeable server to find out more about preparations, which change frequently.

Quail, which on our visit was burnished in aged balsamic, is a standout among the meat and fish options; it went extremely well with a side of sauteed broccoli rabe. Vegetables are handled with utmost care, whether roasted, sautéed or tossed into mixed salads.

Here, they are truly serious about their craft.

CLEAN BITES

- Tom Colicchio received the award for outstanding chef from the James Beard Foundation in 2010.
- Craft supports and gives back to organizations like City Harvest, Children of Bellevue, GrowNYC and HealthRight International, among others.
- Check out Tom's journal at http://www.craftrestaurantsinc.com/toms-journal/.

DARROW'S FARM FRESH TAKEOUT

115 E. 18th St.
212-321-0997

darrowsnyc.com
@DarrowsNYC

Cuisine:
American, Juice bar,
Raw, Vegan, Vegetarian

Neighborhood:
Union Square

Meals Served:
Brunch, Lunch, Dinner

What's in a name? Everything, if you are Darrow's Farm Fresh Takeout. Although we'd also happily call this new Union Square spot "We Want to Eat Lunch Here Every Day."

Darrow's takes a cue from its neighbor and sources as much clean, unprocessed and local food as it can from the Greenmarket.

Start your day with sheep's milk or coconut yogurt and seasonal fruit. Grey mornings that require an infusion of color will benefit from pan-seared peppers with polenta and avocado.

At lunch it's all about the Functional Plates, which are a balanced meal with a nutritional goal (such as stress relief, energy or immunity) in mind: For example, The Immunity Plate is a striking mix of black rice with kabocha squash, roasted carrots and broccolini.

Darrow's is casual enough for a lunch meeting, but sleek enough for a pre-dinner boozy cocktail with cold-pressed juice while oohing and ahhing at the living wall upstairs.

CLEAN BITES

- Save time by ordering ahead of time online.
- Self-service iPads at every table speed up the ordering process. When you settle on what you want (no easy feat), your order is sent directly to the kitchen and you can pay whenever you'd like.
- Keep your eyes out for the cute cow that sporadically makes an appearance on the screen near the in-house market.

DIG INN SEASONAL MARKET

Multiple locations   diginn.com
                            @diginn

Quality sourcing, seasonal ingredients and tasty food are the focus at Dig Inn. No surprise, then, that most days the line's out the door during the lunch rush (it moves quickly).

Diners can choose from sandwiches, salads or "marketplates" with hormone- and antibiotic-free proteins served with two sides on a bed of grains or greens.

Raw, cold-pressed juices, smoothies and shakes are made to order with chia seed, flax seed, soy milk or SunWarrior vegan protein. We like the pomegranate pear smoothie with extra mint—but hold the agave to avoid the cloying sweetness.

Dig Inn's customizable menu offers carnivorous options, while vegetarians can fill up on organic tofu and protein-rich quinoa and everyone can benefit from a veggie overload with the sides. With locations throughout the city, delivery available and economical prices, Dig Inn gives every New Yorker access to a healthy and satisfying meal.

CLEAN BITES

- Must try: "Mom's" braised beef, cooked to perfection in oregano and appealingly astringent red wine vinegar.
- Seasonal specials here are standouts, like a mayo-free wild salmon salad with moist, miso-marinated salmon, diced cucumbers and sweet red bell peppers.
- Nutrition and allergen information is highlighted on their website.

DIMES

49 Canal St.
212-925-1300

dimesnyc.com
@dimestimes

$$

Cuisine:
American
(Contemporary),
Californian

Neighborhood:
Lower East Side

Meals Served:
Breakfast, Brunch,
Lunch, Dinner

Sabrina De Sousa and Alissa Wagner blend California cool
with New York Greenmarket crunch at this expanded
neighborhood café. Standing in line alongside the coolest hipsters
in Manhattan wearing wood-framed glasses, neon socks and dangly
bacon earrings is not something we entertain often, but when we do, it
is at the new Dimes location. With dishes as eccentric as the crowd, we
had trouble choosing between the spiced quinoa with ginger turmeric
hummus or the "big salad" loaded with pickled mustard seeds, candy
cane beets and plum... so we ordered both.

Be sure to return the next morning for a nutrient-dense brunch
and try a refreshing açai bowl that you can top with floral lavender and
blueberries or decadent carob, dates and nutty almond walnut hemp
granola. Coffee-drinkers should cool down their cup with a splash of
the house-made almond milk, which is just one of many reasons why
we'll be returning. See you and your neon socks there!

CLEAN BITES

- Must try: seared tuna nori wrap stuffed with sesame pickled lychee,
  black rice, chili cucumber, avocado and daikon. Like sushi without
  the splinter-finger chopsticks.
- All in-house water is filtered.
- Check out their instagram (@dimestimes) for quirky, colorful posts.

Cuisine:
American
(Contemporary)

Neighborhood:
Williamsburg

Meals Served:
Brunch, Lunch, Dinner

DINER

85 Broadway Ave.   dinernyc.com
718-486-3077

The food changes so regularly at Diner (based on the seasons, availability of goods at the market and the kitchen's whims), that the management doesn't even print menus. Instead, your server writes it on the paper tablecloth as he or she speaks. It's a fun gimmick to a meal that is full of food both simple and extraordinary.

The burger (we would nominate it for one of the best in all the city) is the only menu constant, and the meat is ground nightly. On other nights you might find a brined half chicken with ginger-glazed carrots or bonito boosted by a sweet carrot puree and pickled vegetable salad.

Although both the diner car setting and the beautiful crowd makes a meal here feel trendy and somehow impromptu, Diner has been open since 1998—a lifetime in the vicious cycle of NYC restaurants. Come hungry and enjoy the conscious indulgences.

CLEAN BITES

- Must try: the burger. Really.
- Owner Andrew Tarlow also owns Marlow & Sons (see p. 128), Reynard (see p. 147) and Roman's in Fort Greene (see p. 149).
- Check out Diner Journal, an independent magazine featuring art, literature and recipes that Diner has self-published sine 2006.

DIRTY BIRD TO-GO

155 Chambers St.
212-964-3284

dirtybirdtogo.com
@DirtyBirdToGo

Cuisine:
American (Casual),
Southern

Neighborhood:
Tribeca, Chelsea

Meals Served:
Lunch, Dinner

204 W. 14th St.
212-620-4836

Only in New York can you snag an order from a fried chicken joint and realize—after sinking your teeth into a crisp-skinned, slow-roasted rotisserie bird or an astoundingly juicy fried drumstick—that this is grub from a James Beard Award winner. Former Dirty Bird owner and recipe developer Allison Vines-Rushing has worked with international restaurateur Alain Ducasse, and a simple bite reveals her vast skills.

The fare this chicken joint is turning out is, believe it or not, good for you. Of course, rotisserie chicken is a healthier choice than the crispy stuff (which is soaked in buttermilk and fried in peanut oil), but every Dirty Bird sent out the door is hormone- and antibiotic-free and locally raised. And if you go for the fried stuff, the oil they use for frying is recycled for biodiesel fuel. Sin with a side of sautéed garlic kale—it's excellent here, locally grown and dotted with chili peppers and garlic.

Although this is a chicken joint, it has a large selection of salads and veggie sides to add an antioxidant boost to your meal.

CLEAN BITES

- Dirty Birds are humanely raised in Pennsylvania Amish Country, veggie fed and antibiotic free.
- For some lighter fare, opt for the rotisserie chicken.

Cuisine:
Italian

Neighborhood:
Flatiron

Meals Served:
Breakfast, Lunch,
Dinner

EATALY

200 5th Ave.
212-229-2560

eataly.com/nyc
@Eataly

Everyone who enters this culinary emporium, even the most jaded New York, regresses into a state of doe-eyed fascination the minute he or she crosses the Fifth Avenue threshold. There is so much to consume, both literally and visually, as everything—from the celebrity owners and 50,000-square foot size, to the extensive selection of both hyper-local and imported foods—is over the top.

This glorified warehouse is packed with almost every type of gourmet purveyor imaginable: coffee, gelato, panini, cured meat, fish, fresh pasta, house-made cheese, and pastries, to name a few.

Dining options abound here. Try Manzo, for a more formal experience with table service and a focus on meat. Le Verdure is the vegetable stand (grab a table or bar seat on a first-come, first-serve basis) that features local produce and at least 13 different preparations each day.

On the roof, find Birreria a 4,500-square-foot brewery and restaurant. The 150-seat outdoor oasis features unfiltered, unpasteurized and naturally carbonated ales brewed on-site, and a menu blending locally sourced and imported gourmet foods.

CLEAN BITES

- Must try: Le Verdure's "Verdure alla Piastra"—seasonal vegetables mixed into farro.
- You can purchase *Clean Plates NYC* in the book section!

EL COLMADO BUTCHERY

53 Little W. 12th St.
212-488-0000

elcolmadonyc.com
@ElColmado_NYC

Cuisine:
Juice Bar, Provisions
Shop, Spanish

Neighborhood:
Meatpacking District

Meals Served:
Brunch, Lunch, Dinner

There's a whole lot of good stuff going on at chef Seamus Mullen's Meatpacking District spot: El Colmado Butchery is an upbeat Spanish tapas and wine bar-meets-classic butcher shop. It's also an all-day neighborhood joint where you can wander in for a plate of Serrano ham during the afternoon, pick up pre-High Line picnic provisions, grab an incredible pasture-raised rotisserie chicken for dinner or consult with the butcher about what cut of antibiotic, hormone-free, and responsibly raised meat you should cook at home.

But it's not all meat on the menu here. The night we stopped by we delighted in a bright orange gazpacho made with tomatoes, peppers, cucumber, garlic, olive oil, sherry vinegar and chunks of avocado. In addition, Mullen is an avid green-juice drinker and he offers three fresh-pressed juice blends including the Oro/Gold, which combines pineapple, yellow beet, papaya, lemon and honey.

Never thought you'd be stopping by the neighborhood butcher for a juice infusion, did you?

CLEAN BITES

- Seating at El Colmado Butchery is on a first-come, first-served basis—reservations are not accepted.
- Food from El Colmado Butchery can be delivered through trycaviar. com or the restaurant is happy to prepare food to-go.
- If you love El Colmado Butchery, try the other location of El Colmado in Gotham West Market in Hell's Kitchen.

Cuisine:
American (Traditional)

Neighborhood:
Upper West Side

Meals Served:
Breakfast, Brunch,
Lunch, Dinner

ELIZABETH'S NEIGHBORHOOD TABLE

680 Columbus Ave.   elizabethsnyc.com
212-280-6500

Elizabeth's Neighborhood Table adds some suburban flair to the Upper West Side with a lemony exterior and picturesque white picket fence. Inside, a restaurant and bar with a casual American feel serves up thoughtful comfort food.

A hearty appetizer selection included grass-fed beef sliders, chicken wings and steamed mussels. For the house salad, a simple mesclun mix from the North Fork's Satur Farm is dotted with slices of radish and long thin ribbons of carrots and dressed with sherry-lime vinaigrette. The satisfying veggie burger is packed with grains and vegetables like onions and shredded carrots. It comes with avocado and sunflower sprouts, all served on hearty wheat toast with a side of salad and organic ketchup.

Large portions and the casual restaurant decor may call to mind your average neighborhood spot, but at Elizabeth's meats are all local and hormone- and antibiotic-free, beef is grass-fed, salmon is sustainable, the produce is often organic, and the dishes are satisfying.

CLEAN BITES

- Elizabeth's sources the bulk of its ingredients from Finger Lakes Farms in Ithaca.
- They offer a morning yoga class on their beautiful front porch.

ELLARY'S GREENS

33 Carmine St.
212-920-5072

ellarysgreens.com
@ellarysgreens

Cuisine:
American
(Contemporary)

Neighborhood:
West Village

Meals Served:
Breakfast, Brunch,
Lunch, Dinner

Tucked away on Carmine Street, Ellary's Greens is bringing healthy and affordable gourmet dining to the West Village. The ingredients used in this contemporary cafe are local, organic, and/or natural, with an emphasis on quality and nutrition.

Start with one of the daily soup selections or fresh salads, like nori seaweed with sliced cucumber, daikon and napa cabbage dressed with a citrus vinaigrette. Vietnamese brown rice noodles tossed with halved poached shrimp and egg ribbons in garlicky Nuoc Cham sauce are a refreshing gluten-free pasta alternative.

Refreshments range from cold-pressed juices and Brooklyn-brewed kombucha and cider to biodynamic wine and gluten-free beers. Early risers can wake up to Ellary's weekday breakfast with cage-free eggs and tofu scramble, house-made baked goods and almond spelt pancakes with blueberries and coconut cream.

CLEAN BITES

- The expansive menu employs symbols to denote vegan, vegetarian, dairy-free and gluten-free items.
- Check out Ellary's website to learn more about its vendors.
- Ellary's offers grab-and-go at Equinox locations.

Cuisine:
Greek

Neighborhood:
Kips Bay

Meals Served:
Lunch, Dinner

EONS GREEK FOOD FOR LIFE

633 2nd Ave.
212-696-1234

eonsgreek.com
@EONSgreekfood

When it comes to doing lunch right, EONS Greek Food for Life has got it down. The food is fresh, organic and reasonably priced, the flavors are authentically Greek and the fast-casual service is quick, and comes with a smile.

Eating at EONS will be familiar to Choose-Your-Own-Adventure diners. Pick your base (pita, rice or organic salad greens), choose your protein (options include hormone- and antibiotic free chicken, grass-fed lamb, sushi-grade wild octopus or wild shrimp), select your vegetable sides and go wild with toppings, if the spirit so moves you. A full meal will run you $9 to $15.

It's like Chipotle went on a dreamy Mediterranean vacation.

EONS sets itself apart from the fast-casual crowd with its attention to detail, like compostable dishware and just the right amount of tang in the tzadziki. For a place that gets you food so speedily, EONS does an impressive job.

CLEAN BITES

- For the ultimate in speed, order ahead online.
- If you need to feed a big group, EONS offers catering.
- Don't be surprised if you see people in scrubs; EONS is a hit with the medical staff at the nearby NYU Langone Medical Center.

EXKI

Multiple Locations
212-447-1874

exkinyc.com
@EXKiNYC

Cuisine:
Fast Food, Belgian,
Sandwiches,
Vegetarian

Neighborhood:
Gramercy

Meals Served:
Breakfast, Lunch,

This Belgium-born company has more than 75 locations in Europe and is settling into New York nicely with two park-side locations—one just off of Madison Square and another by Gramercy.

Touches like compostable grab-and-go packaging, green energy, eco-friendly cleaning supplies and food sourced from local heroes such as antibiotic-free FreeBird chicken, Red Jacket juices, Jasper Hill Farm cheeses and organic SoyBoy tofu make us feel right at home. Anything that isn't consumed during breakfast, lunch or dinner is donated to City Harvest at the end of the day.

While EXKi may have originated across the pond, it has done a great job at infusing these city spots with some American tastes by working with chef Galen Zamarra (of Mas (farmhouse) and Almanac), while retaining charming European touches like magazines and newspapers free for the browsing. It's enough to encourage even the busiest worker bee to linger over a pineapple, cucumber, mint and green tea smoothie made with Palais des Thés tea.

CLEAN BITES

- If you need to feed a crowd, EXKi does catering.
- Look for the vegetable emulsions on tartines, salads and wraps— they are a flavorful and 80% vegetable-based healthier alternative to traditional oil-based dressings.
- EXKi is closed on Saturdays and Sundays.

THE FARM ON ADDERLEY

Cuisine:
American
(Contemporary)

Neighborhood:
Ditmas Park

Meals Served:
Brunch, Lunch, Dinner

1108 Cortelyou Rd.
718-287-3101

thefarmonadderley.com
@FarmOnAdderley

Peer at the tree-lined streets with Victorian homes, and driveways (gasp!) near The Farm on Adderley and you'll realize you are definitely not in Manhattan anymore.

Our waitress enthusiastically helped us narrow down our wish list from the seasonal, sustainable menu. We eased in with an appetizer of baby artichokes with a creamy cashew puree, toasted garlic scapes, pickled celery and fresh parsley.

A not-to-be-missed pasture-raised burger was cooked to juicy perfection, transported to a sturdy English muffin, served with a pickle and delectable fries—both homemade—and an addictive curry mayo for dipping (or spicing up your patty).

Wash your meal down with a harmonious glass of cucumber vodka lemonade (house-made, naturally), and be happy to know that this Farm is not far from home.

CLEAN BITES

- The Farm on Adderley offers a whole slew of fun, innovative events year round, from "Rosé and Rhubarb" nights to learning how to make your own gingerbread house. Check out http://www.thefarmonadderley.com/events.

THE FAT RADISH

17 Orchard St.
212-300-4053

thefatradishnyc.com
@thefatradish

Cuisine:
American
(Contemporary),
British

Neighborhood:
Lower East Side

Meals Served:
Brunch, Lunch, Dinner

The phrase "farm-to-table" has become a favorite of many restaurants, so much so that you might be skeptical of its authenticity. However, The Fat Radish is the real deal.

The aesthetic here is a chic take on industrial-meets-organic, with plenty of worn wood and weathered brick, and the food has no problem standing up to the surroundings.

Try a plate of heirloom carrots served beside a tussle of kale with bits of hijiki seaweed that emit miso-scented steam. The market salad is a study in freshness, a marriage of buttery and bitter flavors enhanced with subtle sesame vinaigrette and avocado.

Pan-seared sea bass arrives snowy white beside market succotash. Rarely does minimalism convey such depth—proteins betray no seasoning but taste and feel satisfying, especially when sprinkled with sea salt from the little bowls atop each table.

CLEAN BITES

- British chef co-owners Ben Towill and Phil Winser also lead Silkstone Events —a full production and catering company.
- During the summer of 2014, Ben Towill went on a cross-country bike tour of more than 4,500 miles to have conversations about food with, as he put it, "total strangers." He also raised over $25,000 for Just Food's Youth Community Chef program.

Cuisine:
Australian

Neighborhood:
Greenpoint

Meals Served:
Breakfast, Lunch,
Dinner

FIVE LEAVES

18 Bedford Ave.
718-383-5345

fiveleavesny.com
@FiveLeavesNY

$$$

Five Leaves has mastered the art of the first impression: charming outdoor tables, a corner location, the unusual '20s-era boiler-room door to the WC. When finally getting a table at this no-reservations restaurant (be prepared to wait at peak times), the list of enticing, responsibly-sourced dishes will seem worth the wait.

The concept here is often called Australian comfort food. Judge for yourself what that means exactly by digging into a big black kale salad energized with spicy anchovy dressing, aged Gouda and hazelnuts.

Also test out the house-made ricotta, topped with fresh figs, thyme, honeycomb, Maldon sea salt, served with warm fruit-nut bread. A few bites of this dish will satisfy any craving for something creamy. Diners with hearty appetites will be drawn to the organic lamb shepherd's pie, served bubbling and topped with honey-roasted root vegetables.

CLEAN BITES

- Must try: the Five Leaves Burger—juicy, grass-fed beef; house pickled beets; harissa mayo; and a sunny-side-up egg with fried pineapple.
- Anytime is a good time to eat at Five Leaves: The restaurant is open daily from 8 a.m. to 1 a.m. and offers an in-between meals menu.

FLATBUSH FARM

76 St. Marks Ave.
718-622-3276

flatbushfarm.com
@Flatbush_Farm

Cuisine:
American
(Contemporary)

Neighborhood:
Park Slope

Meals Served:
Brunch, Lunch, Dinner

Flatbush Farm's backyard garden dining area is so beautiful it belongs in a fairy tale. High trestle walls encompass a vast space that feels simultaneously intimate and like being at a grand party. The indoor dining room is classy and comfortable, but sit outside if you can (and you often can, since it is enormous).

Definitely opt for the Flatbush bread appetizer, served with Mediterranean-inspired purees and tapenades. The salmon with zucchini potato hash and tomato fennel broth is great. Also delicious is the cauliflower steak with quinoa, maitake mushrooms, capers and kale.

Flatbush Farm is good for large groups and parties; the menu has something for everyone. There is a sister bar, cleverly called Bar(n), next door for before or after, and the staff is more than happy to help you celebrate.

CLEAN BITES

- Local purveyors are listed proudly on the restaurant's website.
- In addition to its main menu, Flatbush Farm offers a bar menu, with unique offerings like a veggie burger—a patty packed with quinoa, mushrooms and lentils.

Cuisine:
Italian

Neighborhood:
Carroll Gardens, West Village

Meals Served:
Brunch, Lunch, Dinner

FRANKIES 457

457 Court St.
718-403-0033

frankiesspuntino.com
@franksspuntino

FRANKIES 570

570 Hudson St.
212-924-0818

Frankies is genius. The menu is long and varied, with salads, sandwiches, crostini, pastas, vegetable plates, cheese and charcuterie—but every item is made from carefully chosen, delicious ingredients.

The simple dishes here, prepared with usually two or maybe three ingredients, offer texture and flavor to impressive result. Pine nuts, ricotta, bacon, arugula and polenta all show up in serious preponderance.

The roasted beets and avocados with balsamic vinegar are among the best versions available in the city. The two vegetables are perfectly paired—the fatty avocado and the sweet beets enrich each other, and the acid cuts both in the balsamic vinegar. Vegetable antipasti like the cauliflowers and carrots are roasted to a fleshy perfection, while incredibly rich pine nut polenta is pillowy, with a soft bite from the pine nuts. Don't skip a selection from the pasta menu, like the sweet potato and sage ravioli in a Parmesan broth.

CLEAN BITES

- Frankies makes its own extra-virgin, unfiltered olive oil.

FRANNY'S

348 Flatbush Ave.
718-230-0221

frannysbrooklyn.com
@frannysbk

Cuisine:
Italian

Neighborhood:
Park Slope

Meals Served:
Lunch, Dinner

It is not easy to stand out in a city brimming with gourmet pizza restaurants, but Franny's has figured out how to do it. Here's the recipe:

First, acknowledge your vendors and purveyors by printing their names and contributions on the back of your recycled menu.

Second, champion unfailingly simple flavor combinations: crostino with wood-roasted corn, peppers and squash butter or try the pizza with zucchini, squash blossoms, anchovies, garlic, basil and buffalo mozzarella.

Third, treat waiting guests (you almost always have to wait to dine) with forthrightness, quoting actual wait times and making real suggestions about other places to go (when dining at Franny's isn't going to happen for them in a timely manner.)

Snag a table here and it's hard to go wrong with anything. Start with vegetables, like a generous portion of the lettuce and herb salad, move on to the uniformly excellent pizzas and finish with chocolate sorbet.

CLEAN BITES

- If you like Franny's, try their sister bar and grill Rose's right down the street.
- Franny's uses renewable energy, made up of 35% wind power and 65% small hydroelectric power; Tri-State Biodiesel converts their kitchen grease to biodiesel fuel.

Cuisine:
American
(Contemporary)

Neighborhood:
Gramercy

Meals Served:
Lunch, Dinner

GRAMERCY TAVERN

42 E. 20th St.
212-477-0777

gramercytavern.com
@GramercyTavern

This member of Danny Meyer's coterie occupies a sedate stretch just north of shopper-packed Union Square. The eatery has received renewed attention since chef Michael Anthony took the helm in 2006, and with a focus on knowing its farmers, ensuring sustainable use of animals, and local, mostly organic produce, it deserves it.

Two restaurants essentially cohabit one awning: Up front is the casual Tavern, featuring broad, blowsy murals of cabbages and onions, and a long, wooden bar. Profusions of spectacular flowers in the foyer change weekly from bright sunflowers to elegant roses. The more formal Dining Room features Impressionist-era portraits, so this is definitely where we'll bring Mom when she's in town.

Anthony's fare is solidly and elegantly American, and completely delicious. Start with the simple, but perfect summer greens, with fingerling potatoes, pancetta and buttermilk dressing followed by smoked Arctic char, corn, shishito peppers and peaches. Even if you skip dessert, sweet farewells from the charming hostess will follow you out the door—yet another reason Mom will love it.

CLEAN BITES

- Chef Michael Anthony is an active presence on Twitter. Follow him @chefmikeanthony to see what he is picking up at market.

THE GREEN TABLE

75 9th Ave.
212- 741- 6623

cleaverco.com
@GreenTableNYC

Cuisine:
American
(Casual)

Neighborhood:
Chelsea

Meals Served:
Brunch, Lunch, Dinner

Chelsea Market's echoing, industrial hallways are crammed with row after row of artisanal food purveyors such as beloved local Amy's Breads or the excellent butcher Dickson's Farmstand Meats (p. 176). But one of the market's longest-standing and best inhabitants is The Green Table.

Owner Mary Cleaver is devoted to organic ingredients, local family farms and sustainable agriculture and her daily-changing menu of fresh, seasonal American classics reflects that. There is a heartbreakingly tasty burger served on roll from Amy's and lavished with kimchi, bacon and tomato relish.

There's also a great free-range chicken pot pie on offer that shouldn't be missed. Break the shiny, crackly pâte brisée crust to reveal moist slices of dark meat, corn and peas in a savory broth.

Downtown in Battery Park, Table Green features local beer and wine on tap, grilled sandwiches, harvest salads made with produce from the Battery Urban Farm, while Table Green Café offers Brooklyn Roasting Crop-to-Cup coffee and espresso, ready to eat sandwiches, hand made pastries and cookies.

CLEAN BITES

- The chicken potpie at The Green Table is also available frozen for takeaway.
- The bar is open all day at The Green Table and Happy Hour is from to 4 to 7 p.m. on weekdays.

HOME

Cuisine:
American
(Contemporary)

Neighborhood:
Greenwich Village

Meals Served:
Brunch, Lunch, Dinner

20 Cornelia St.
212-243-9579

homerestaurantnyc.com
@HomeNYC

With just 30 seats, Home is a real neighborhood charmer tucked into a tiny space.

Locals dine on the small back patio under the canopy of trees and the backs of brownstones. The menu is Contemporary American, showcasing local, sustainable, and seasonal ingredients—it reads like a road map up the coast with stops in Hudson Valley, Lake Placid and Nantucket.

The menu is meat-heavy, but built on perfectly cooked and seasoned vegetables, which sometimes outshine the meat. Eggplant steak with barley, legumes, charred ramps and fiddlehead ferns is a deliciously substantial vegetarian option. Carnivores will be happy with the full-flavored and grass-fed New York strip steak.

The all-American wine list is heavy on New York vintages and features a few biodynamic bottles and by-the-glass selections. After your meal, there's a plate of homemade chocolate chip cookies to nibble on your way out—just like home.

CLEAN BITES

- Must try: the Earl's Palmer.
- Home showcases their seasonal specialties right on the home page of their website.
- Their cocktails are enhanced with homemade (pun intended) infustions.
- Home has a beautiful garden patio.

HU KITCHEN

78 5th Ave.
212-510-8919

hukitchen.com
@HuKitchen

Cuisine:
American (Casual)

Neighborhood:
Union Square

Meals Served:
Breakfast, Lunch,
Dinner

Whether you are into the Paleo diet or not, this spot offers some damn good food with an entirely gluten-free menu of nutritious foods sans dairy and grains (unless noted).

Early morning options include a make-your-own breakfast mashbar that is served all day with chia seed pudding, fruit and nut toppings and freshly baked gluten-free muffins.

A made-to-order meal area touts pastured meats and organic vegetables. Create your own mix-and-match bowl by selecting a base of organic quinoa, root vegetable mash or a raw veggie medley and top it off with roasted wild mushrooms, grass-fed ground beef or robust organic Moroccan chicken flavored with onion, garlic, ginger, coriander and cumin.

Crisp-skinned, hormone-free rotisserie chicken brined in sea salt and dusted with organic coconut sugar is a perennial standout.

With so many flavor options and high-quality ingredients, "getting back to a more human way of eating" never tasted so good.

CLEAN BITES

- Must try: crunchy banana chocolate bar. Hu makes its own chocolate, which is sweetened with low-glycemic coconut palm sugar.
- The restaurant makes its own condiments, so no need to dip those almond-crusted organic chicken fingers in corn syrup-infested ketchup!
- Hu is 100% GMO-free.

Cuisine:
American
(Contemporary)

Neighborhood:
Soho

Meals Served:
Breakfast, Brunch,
Lunch, Dinner

HUNDRED ACRES

38 Macdougal St.
212-475-7500

hundredacresnyc.com
@hundredacresnyc

This Soho restaurant is helmed by the same husband-and-wife team behind Cookshop (p. 92) and Vic's (p. 163) and (thankfully!) the same strong desire to source locally and seasonally.

The trendy eatery sports a see-and-be-seen bar area, with a dining room up front. Japanese-inspired lanterns hang overhead, French windows open to the street and a sociable buzz dominates. If you are looking for quiet, the back room or petite garden might be better for a sedate evening out.

While the vibe is buzzy, the food embraces a clean, unpretentious approach to flavor. Healthy omnivores will delight in the many choices for organic chicken, grass-fed beef and fish. There are plenty of vegetable options, like braised collard greens, for those who don't eat meat. Sea salt graces the table, but happily, none of the food—whether pan roasted trout with fava bean-summer squash-sweet corn succotash or a roasted Berkshire ham with bourbon and blueberries—requires it.

CLEAN BITES

- Must try: brunch. The restaurant makes its granola in-house and offers goat-cheese bread pudding.
- Hundred Acres has a $24 prix-fixe market-driven lunch.

IL BUCO

47 Bond St. ilbuco.com
212-533-1932 @ilbuconyc

IL BUCO ALIMENTARI & VINERIA

53 Great Jones St. ilbucovineria.com
212-837-2622 @IlBuco_AV

Cuisine:
Italian

Neighborhood:
Noho

Meals Served:
Breakfast (A & V),
Brunch (A & V), Lunch,
Dinner

An out-of-towner calls and demands a proper introduction to the city—someplace "chic and very New York." Take him to Il Buco.

The Italian eatery is almost dauntingly Old World, imbuing the throwaway adjectives "beautiful" and "romantic" with real meaning via a visual cacophony of hanging copper pots, dark wooden antiques and profusions of flowers.

A huge square of lasagna conceals spicy organic beef, kale and heady Taleggio amidst its folds. A vegetable "carpaccio" of razor-thin zucchini and squash impresses with a jolt of citrus juice, sparkles of mint and curls of salty Parmesan. Fill up on sides of snappily fresh peas and soft white beans, because there is plenty of house-cured pork to go around.

Raucous younger sister Il Buco Alimentari & Vineria boasts a small grocery with carefully curated dry goods, meats, breads, gelato and pastry up front and a jovial restaurant in the back.

CLEAN BITES

- Fun fact: Il Buco started as an antique store with a small kitchen in the back.
- Check both websites to see a list of purveyors.
- Il Buco gets high marks for using only sea salt and olive oil in the kitchen. In fact, the restaurant hosts a Fall Harvest Olive Oil tasting every year.

Cuisine:
American
(Contemporary)

Neighborhood:
Williamsburg

Meals Served:
Brunch, Lunch, Dinner

ISA

348 Wythe Ave.
347-689-3594

isa.gg
@IsaWythe

$$$

Isa is terribly alluring. The décor here manages to be rustic without becoming another country-chic cliché. Here, triangles rule, patterning the wooden beams on the ceiling and fusing into diamonds on the door. Even the light fixtures are hexagonal.

What really makes the food at Isa stand out is that it's cooked in an open, wood-fired oven. If charring thrills you, look for it on the grilled skirt steak, one of the city's best. Sliced on a wooden board, it was blackened to juicy satisfaction. The oven-roasted porgy was likewise crispy, simple and generous. Served whole with nothing but a lemon, this was the kind of large, fresh and honest seafood one rarely finds outside the Mediterranean. Warm vegetable sides including eggplant, ember-cooked to melty softness and hot with chili flakes, round out the a la carte options.

Hip up to its rafters, Isa still manages to be approachable and friendly, a warm neighborhood joint.

CLEAN BITES

- The second floor of the restaurant serves as an event space for everything from DJ parties to herb planting workshops.
- Isa runs a happy hour daily from 4 to 7 p.m.

118

KAFFE 1668

Multiple locations   kaffe1668.com
@kaffe1668

Cuisine:
American (Casual)

Meals Served:
Breakfast, Lunch

When it comes to grab-and-go breakfasts, the usual coffee shop options — doughnuts, croissants, bagels — tend not to qualify as healthy Kaffe 1668, however, takes the guilt out of the morning rush.

The shop focuses on healthy, locally sourced dishes, starting with breakfasts of raw, homemade, steel-cut oatmeal, a baguette with pasture-raised ham and local butter, and local Greek yogurt with figs, pecans and maple syrup.

The enticements carry on throughout the day. The aptly named Healing Bowl is a treasure chest of healthy ingredients, including organic tempeh, beans, quinoa and vegetables in a tahini-miso-ginger dressing. Vegetable-packed salads are named for their antioxidant, alkalizing and vitality-enriching properties.

The menu includes whole-wheat or gluten-free sandwiches and wraps and even a meatball marinara sandwich, made with grass-fed beef, pasture-raised turkey or organic tofu balls. Finish the meal with a cup of the coffee that started it all. The shop roasts its single-origin, fair-trade beans nearby in Red Hook, Brooklyn.

CLEAN BITES

- A refrigerated case up front lets harried diners pick up cold-pressed juices, salads and chilled portions of the house specials, like semolina lasagna with grass-fed beef.

Cuisine:
Eastern European

Neighborhood:
Cobble Hill

Meals Served:
Brunch, Lunch, Dinner

KARLOFF

254 Court St.
347-689-4279

karloffnyc.com
@Karloff_Bk

What's sweeter than affordable, "seasonal comfort food" in an uncramped Cobble Hill cafe? The people behind it. Beside a small, smiling staff, Karloff co-owner Olga Shishko lifts spirits and nourishes bodies with her warm demeanor and home-style Eastern European cooking.

The comfortable dining area and local, organic coffee and ice cream entices lingering lunchers, but cool nights are the best time to soothe your belly at Karloff.

Seasonal ingredients dictate Karloff's clipboard- and chalkboard-displayed offerings. Wash down a kale and collard greens soup with broccoli puree with a glass of complimentary cucumber water. Local, sustainable meats carry the mains, although pescetarians can count on a healthy grilled fish entrée, and everyone should try the vegan borscht.

Karloff's specialty beverages, like organic kefir smoothies, provide alternatives to dessert. We opted for kampot, a cool, straw-and-spoon-worthy sugar-free soup. Like the rest of the meal, it packed a punch (here, of the fruit variety) without being overly decadent. Few things could be sweeter.

CLEAN BITES

- Want a drink? Karloff infuses vodka with local and organic herbs and fruits.
- Karloff takes great pride (as they well should!) in participating in a numerous charity events. Check out the home page of their website for a full listing.

LEFT BANK

117 Perry St.
212-727-1170

leftbanknewyork.com
@leftbanknyc

Cuisine:
American
(Contemporary)

Neighborhood:
West Village

Meals Served:
Dinner

$$$

After several NYC credits to his name, chef Laurence Edelman opened Left Bank in 2011 with two food goals in mind: to source humanely raised meat and to get the best produce out there. His battle cry? Buy food from people you know!

This modern West Village tavern does just that, offering European-influenced Contemporary American fare focused on in-season produce, sustainable seafood and meats, and local ingredients.

The ever-changing menu consists of simply executed dishes that let the ingredients shine, like gnocchi with sugar snaps and summer squash, and iron-roasted chicken with delicately crisped skin and a juicy interior—both excellent entrées.

Seasonal vegetables are particular standouts: crisp Jersey flat beans dressed in honey dijon, and cauliflower florets get roasted and tossed with shallots and harissa.

Inspired by the creative culture of the Village itself, this welcoming neighborhood gem will quickly become your new go-to.

CLEAN BITES

- Left Bank screens classic movies during Sundays in the summer, and chef Edelman prepares a special menu of dishes and cocktails inspired by each film.
- Any of the artwork catch your eye? Left Bank features a rotating collection of paintings and photographs curated by local artists—often available for purchase.
- Every day from 5 to 7 p.m. there is a Happy Hour special: $25 for an appetizer and pasta dish.

Cuisine:
American
(Contemporary)

Neighborhood:
Williamsburg

Meals Served:
Brunch, Dinner

THE LIGHTHOUSE

145 Borinquen Pl.
347-789-7742

lighthousebk.com
@lighthousebk

You might have heard about the Big Salad at The Lighthouse. We can confirm: It is huge and delicious, and while it doesn't have everything, everything it has, you want. Walnuts and red onion are daintily distributed among a generous portion of arugula, beet, carrot, cucumber and radish. The balance is perfect, and the mustard vinaigrette brings it all together.

The Lighthouse touts its raw bar for good reason. Each day brings a ceviche, tartare and local oyster selection with a variety of mignonettes and sauces.

The Israeli-born brother and sister team that own the restaurant allow their native food culture to seep through with heaps of vibrant ingredients like parsley, garlic, aioli and yogurt and in dishes like the brunch shakshuka of spiced tomatoes, poached eggs and tahini.

Dishes here taste likes ones the chef would make for his family; while you're dining, you almost feel as though you are.

CLEAN BITES

- Why the name Lighthouse? The windowed dining room here allows for 180-degree visibility.

THE LITTLE BEET

135 W. 50th St.

212-459-2338

thelittlebeet.com

@littlebeet

THE LITTLE BEET TABLE

333 Park Ave. S.

212-466-3330

thelittlebeettable.com

@littlebeettable

Cuisine:
American (Casual)

Neighborhood:
Midtown West, Flatiron

Meals Served:
Breakfast, Lunch,
Dinner

Who knew you could find a fast-casual eatery offering fresh, seasonal food in the heart of Midtown?

The Little Beet has one simple philosophy: to serve real food, deliciously. Step in line for hearty proteins cooked on the plancha—chicken, salmon, beef and tofu—all sourced from top-notch local farms and served with a rotating selection of leafy salads and vegetable sides. Early risers can kick-start their day with cold-pressed juices in sweet and savory blends, organic egg whites, kale and onions in a brown rice wrap, or raw oatmeal topped with fresh berries and homemade jam.

At spinoff The Little Beet Table, the menu is still gluten-free and just as focused on the top-notch ingredients, but the chic setting and the full-service, sit-down menu make it more suitable for a considered dinner out. There are also cocktails, biodynamic wines and gluten-free beers.

CLEAN BITES

- All of The Little Beet's menu items are 100% gluten-free.

LITTLE PARK

85 W. Broadway
212-220-4110

littlepark.com
@littleparknyc

$$$

While chef Andrew Carmellini has always been concerned with sourcing and seasonal cooking, Little Park is his first restaurant to focus exclusively on highlighting organic, sustainable ingredients and highlighting products from local farmers, anglers, vintners and foragers.

We were overjoyed to see that vegetable and grain dishes get just as much love on the menu as their more meaty counterparts here. Vegetable options even outweigh the fire-roasted meats 2 to 1, inlcuding the excellent grass-fed hanger steak with charred broccoli.

Servers are knowledgeable about the components of each dish—yes, you'll be told, that's a hint of yuzu in the buttery Peconic Bay Scallops joined by a Gold Rush variety apple and those tiny dots are poppy seeds sprinkled over the beetroot risotto.

Look to that hearty vegetable section to be introduced to uncommon picks, like the heirloom radicchio salad with bits of fennel and an orange-anchovy dressing.

CLEAN BITES

- Little Park is located in the Smyth Hotel.
- If you can't get a reservation, you can walk-in and enjoy full-service dining at the bar.
- If you like the Little Park vibe, try some of Andrew Carmellini's other restaurants like The Dutch, Lafayette, Locanda Verde and Bar Primi.

LYFE KITCHEN

248 W. 55th St.
212-265-5933

lyfekitchen.com
@LYFEKitchen

Cuisine:
American (Casual),
Fast Food, Juice Bar,
Vegan, Vegetarian

Neighborhood:
Midtown

Meals Served:
Breakfast, Lunch,
Dinner

Lyfe Kitchen has found the sweet spot on the intersection of healthfulness and affordability, while maintaining convenient hours and speedy service. The fast-casual chain balances pricing by carefully choosing produce from the Dirty Dozen and Clean Fifteen lists, while sticking with antibiotic-free meats and eggs from cage-free chickens.

You'll never have a question about what you're eating, whether it's a grass-fed beef burger or a quinoa crunch wrap with local vegetables. Lyfe Kitchen proudly displays a full ingredient list, as well as calorie, sodium and nut-allergy information. Paleo, gluten-free, vegetarian and vegan eaters are all well covered here.

Smoothies and tasty drinks won't leave you clutching your wallet; libations like a ginger mint chia water or a kale banana smoothie are particularly well priced.

The first floor seating may be convenient, but space and natural light can be found overhead. Grab a table upstairs when you are done ordering and your food will be brought up to you.

CLEAN BITES

- Lyfe offers lightning-quick service, but to really make things fly order ahead of time online. Delivery is also available.
- The chain's owners were once chefs to single name greats like Ellen and Oprah.
- Lyfe offers catering if you need to feed a crowd.

Cuisine:
Bakery, French,
Sandwiches, Salad Bar

Neighborhood:
Soho

Meals Served:
Breakfast, Lunch

MAMAN BAKERY & CAFÉ

239 Centre St.
212-226-0770

mamannyc.com
@ _mamannyc_

PAPA POULE

189 Lafayette St.
212-226-8726

papapoulenyc.com

On any given day, whatever simple comforts are coming out of Maman's open kitchen are sure to be healthful, radiant in color and made with a dose of classic French technique.

The South of France-inspired bakery and café evokes meals prepared by a doting French mother. The team conjures dishes like red rice salad with a sweet and sour eggplant ratatouille, pear and parsnip soup, and chickpea salad with roasted pumpkin, beets and an orange-honey vinaigrette.

A couple blocks away at the itty-bitty takeout joint and brother restaurant Papa Poule, the glorious smell of chickens will practically knock you out.

The team sources organic, free-range Québécoise birds. Once the birds land in the shop, they are marinated with olive oil and massaged with a heavy dose of garlic, thyme, and rosemary before being putting on the rotisserie for a bombastically flavorful result. Salads loaded with local produce, homemade pitas and chicken and egg breakfast items are also available.

CLEAN BITES

- Maman and Papa Poule offer their menu items for dine-in, carryout, catering or delivery.

MANA

646 Amsterdam Ave.

manarestaurantnyc.com

212-787-1110

Cuisine:
Asian, Macrobiotic

Neighborhood:
Upper West Side

Meals Served:
Brunch, Lunch, Dinner

Buoyantly friendly service, organic bottles of wine and Asian-inflected fare are the unexpected hallmarks of this spot. The grub is good, the water filtered, and the organic, macrobiotic, vegetarian and vegan-focused menu is a gem—it's easy to see why it's a neighborhood standby.

An aromatic miso-based kelp vegetable soup delivers a hearty oomph via a few skinny wood ear mushrooms, and okonomoyaki—our cheery waiter laughed as we struggled to pronounce it—a savory Japanese buckwheat pancake is delicately fried and served with sundried tomato sauce.

Pescatarians will delight in the bevy of fish options, but perhaps the best part of dining here are the many vegetable options, like bok choy and broccoli sautéed with ginger and garlic.

As you clear your plate, look around the spic-and-span joint, let the owner know how you liked the fare (she often tours the room) and note that she is cleaning the tables herself. It's just that sort of place.

CLEAN BITES

- Must try: curried sweet potato dumplings.
- Desserts, like the adzuki almond mousse and the tofu cheesecake, are always prepared without dairy or sugar.

Cuisine:
American
(Contemporary)

Neighborhood:
Williamsburg

Meals Served:
Breakfast, Lunch,
Dinner

MARLOW & SONS

81 Broadway Ave. marlowandsons.com
718-384-1441

The constantly changing menu here is simple, informative and functional. It's one page, and it serves as your placemat, describing dishes in a super-minimalist manner: "tomatoes" and "halibut." The service at Marlow & Sons is fantastic—efficient, educated, friendly and passionate—so don't hesitate to ask for more details.

A menu constant here is the famous "brick chicken." A breast and thigh are par-cooked under a brick until flattened and crisp and then finished in a saucepan, resulting in a perfectly done chicken.

Many of the wines at Marlow & Sons are organic, biodynamic and unfiltered, yielding a wayward list of old world wines that pair uncannily well with the always flavorful food.

CLEAN BITES

- Don't have time to dine? Stop by the front room for coffee, baked goods and a curated selection of artisanal goods to-go.
- No part unused: The Marlow & Sons team makes gorgeous leather goods from the skin of cows used in the restaurant (really). Check them out at marlowgoods.com.
- Marlow & Sons is brought to you by the same owner as Diner (p. 98), Reynard (p. 147) and Romans (p. 149).

MAS (FARMHOUSE)

39 Downing St. masfarmhouse.com
212-255-1790 @Masfarmhouse

Cuisine:
American
(Contemporary),
French

Neighborhood:
West Village

Meals Served:
Dinner

If you ever find yourself wandering around like Little Red Riding Hood on her way to grandmothers, through the woods of the West Village in search of a French farmhouse, be sure to meander past Downing Street. Push through the enchantingly heavy wooden door at Mas that glows from within and a friendly hostess will greet you with a charming smile.

After learning of Chef Galen Zamarra's commitment to sourcing by the season, every dish seemed to "follow nature's lead." We started off indulgently with complex, earthy chanterelles that are brought to life with spicy arugula and zingy fennel, all held together with a deviled quail egg.

Continuing the mushroom theme, our entrée of zesty goat cheese ravioli was sprinkled with maitakes over a pleasantly light pea puree and parmesan foam. The grand finale of the evening was dessert (sans mushrooms this time): Summer comes to life when stripes of green zucchini sweep across moist cake filled with basil cream that blends beautifully into sautéed peaches. Cleanse your mouth with a spoonful of the chamomile ice cream and repeat.

CLEAN BITES

- Must try: artisanal domestic cheese selection with (or in place of) dessert.
- For a special night out, try the tasting menu that comes with an optional wine pairing.
- There is a distinct focus on sustainable, organic and biodynamic wine.

THE MERMAID INN

Multiple locations

themermaidnyc.com
@themermaidnyc

Cuisine:
Seafood

Neighborhood:
Upper West Side, East
Village, Greenwich
Village

Meals Served:
Brunch, Dinner

 $$$

If you've got a hankering for fresh fish, The Mermaid Inn is where you should point your compass.

All three locations are often jam-packed, and once you get a taste of the classic seafood specialties and a feel for the relaxed vibe, you'll get what all the fuss is about.

Start with selections from the raw bar (think briny East Coast oysters, Littleneck clams and classic shrimp cocktail) and move on to fun twists on New England favorites like lobster and corn fritters with maple and truffle honey, fried clam sliders and a lobster roll served on brioche that is talked about all over the city. The Mermaid Inn does its part to seeks out responsible fisheries and promotes sustainable and local seafood.

For those who want to take a lighter tack, there are plenty of small plates, like a tomato gazpacho with microgreens and a kale salad decked out with white anchovies, capers and shaved Parmesan.

CLEAN BITES

- The Mermaid Inn has its own app: Oysterpedia. It was designed to take the guesswork out of ordering oysters as well as to provide a reference tool for the oysters you have
- Share the American fish love: Gift cards are available.

MESA COYOACAN

372 Graham Ave.   mesacoyoacan.com
718-782-8171   @MesaCoyoacan

Cuisine:
Mexican

Neighborhood:
Williamsburg

Meals Served:
Brunch, Lunch, Dinner

Named for the area of Mexico City where chef Ivan Garcia grew up, this authentic Mexican cocina honors the region's culinary classics with recipes handed down by Garcia's grandmother.

The restaurant's industrial-looking Graham Avenue facade disguises an inviting interior that features a medley of tables and pop music bouncing off the walls.

With a focus on organic ingredients and quality proteins, the menu offers plenty of healthy choices, including a ceviche of tender octopus, grilled corn, avocado, pico de gallo and orange slices. Tiny handmade tortillas (three tacos to an order) are topped with spit-grilled chunks of marinated grass-fed beef, chopped onions and cilantro.

Chiles en nogada—roasted poblano pepper stuffed with shredded Berkshire pork, pears, apples, peaches and almonds, covered with luscious walnut sauce—is a standout.

Grab a date or a group of friends and settle in for some delicious comida that does granny proud.

CLEAN BITES

- Must try: Napal asado grilled cactus with Oaxacan cheese and rajas con crema.
- Check out Mesa Coyoacan's sister restaurant, Zona Rosa (p. 166).
- Quench your thirst: The restaurant is known for its fresh fruit sangria and margaritas made with house-infused tequilas.

Cuisine:
Japanese

Neighborhood:
Williamsburg

Meals Served:
Lunch, Dinner

MOMO SUSHI SHACK

43 Bogart St.
718-418-6666

momosushishack.com
@MomoSushiShack

Not to be mistaken for a member of the David Chang family, this Japanese spot is discreetly housed in a former garage. The sleek, dim space's small size and long communal tables will have you rubbing elbows with Williamsburg's artfully inked arms in no time.

Our first pick from Momo's roster of vegetarian eats was the tofu salad: extraordinarily silky pressed tofu, avocado, local heirloom tomatoes and watercress plated and drizzled with basil-infused soy sauce.

Fish- and vegetable-on-rice "bombs"—think nigiri but rounder—include the tasty Katide Doko Roll, an umami smack of crimini, shitake and avocado.

Pick from three types of soy: classic, slightly spicy and green with wasabi (tamari is available as a gluten-free alternative). Momo is ideal for family-style dining, but this hidden spot is no secret; large groups should be prepared for a (worthwhile) wait.

CLEAN BITES

- Must try: "Ramo" roll with tofu cream cheese, cilantro and chopped vegetables.
- Momo offers yuzu-pickled red cabbage as a fun twist on the classic ginger palate cleanser.
- In addition to the traditional omakase, Momo offers a vegan omakase as well.

MONUMENT LANE

103 Greenwich Ave.
212-255-0155

monumentlane.com
@monumentlane

Cuisine:
American
(Contemporary)

Neighborhood:
West Village

Meals Served:
Brunch, Lunch, Dinner

With its worn-in wood, cushiony barstools, vintage Hudson River maps and Union Jack flag, Monument Lane feels decidedly homespun. The catch? Sophisticated food.

Monument Lane sources from regional, sustainable farms and changes its menu weekly to reflect what's fresh. The menu includes oysters, cheese, butcher boards and snacks—crispy chickpeas and a plate of watermelon with a zing of chili and lime. But we skipped right to the small plates, essentially appetizers for two. The sprout salad is a knockout with pea shoots, sunflower sprouts, butter lettuce, pumpkin seeds and sherry-shallot vinaigrette.

Main courses include the likes of Spanish mackerel with spiced fingerlings, confit red pepper and summer nage, and roasted Goffle Farms chicken, warm bread salad, basil, capers and cherry tomatoes.

To finish the evening, dig into a sweet and simple dessert like blueberry crisp with whipped cream and thyme.

CLEAN BITES

- Monument Lane offers a special $27 three-course Sunday Supper.
- Go for the green: Monument Lane recycles old fryer oil into bio-diesel fuel and composts all organic material.
- The name? Monument Lane is what Greenwich Avenue was originally called.

Cuisine:
American (Casual)

Neighborhood:
Tribeca

Meals Served:
Breakfast, Lunch,
Dinner

MULBERRY & VINE

73 Warren St.   mulberryandvine.com
212-791-6300   @mulberryandvine

"Eat local, cook global" and "Real food, big flavor, no dieting!" are the mantras at Mulberry & Vine, and we love them both.

Health-conscious eaters can drop by the walk-up counter for internationally inspired food, served all day. Dairy, eggs and tofu are organic and local; grains and greens too, when possible and in season. All poultry and meats are hormone- and antibiotic-free. Sauces and dressings are made in-house, without preservatives. Instead of loading up on fats and oils, the kitchen uses local pesticide-free herbs and spices to elevate flavors.

Ordering your meal is simple: Select any combination of the prepared hot and cold dishes. Then, add a bed of seasonal greens or one of the daily soups, like chipotle gazpacho or African tomato curry. The signature skin-on roasted chicken seasoned with lemon and rosemary is juicy and robust, but the carnitas with thinly sliced vegetables and a peppery tomatillo Poblano yogurt sauce is a star.

A slew of prepared salads and snacks like homemade curried cashews are available to grab on-the-go. Beverage options include blended fruit and veggie juices from LuliTonix, Toby's Estate coffee and Copper Sky wine.

CLEAN BITES

- Be sure to inquire about the daily farmers market specials.
- Check out the tables—they are made from reclaimed wood.

NARCISSA

25 Cooper Sq.
212-228-3344

narcissarestaurant.com

Cuisine:
American
(Contemporary)

Neighborhood:
East Village

Meals Served:
Brunch, Lunch, Dinner

Narcissa's namesake is a cow at owner Andre Balazs' upstate farm, but aside from thoughtfully procured ingredients there's little hint of farm life here. Nor is there the feeling that you're in a hotel restaurant. Although housed in The Standard East Village, Narcissa attracts sleek Manhattanites vying for a table in the serene backyard space.

If the weather doesn't permit an al fresco experience, Narcissa has two distinct dining rooms. The main dining room offers a more intimate experience, or you can dine with the chefs in the other as Narcissa brings "open kitchen" to a whole new level—you can actually sit at the food prep station as if it were a sushi bar.

Straight-from-the-farm flavor combinations stud the menu, like carrot and jalapeno; beet, apple and horseradish; and strawberries and gouda. The menu changes seasonally, but we especially relished the near perfect creamy goodness and peppery finish of the potato gnocchi with garbanzo beans and morel mushrooms. The heat of the spicy sofrito kale was well balanced by the woodiness of the accompanying shiitakes and the tenderness of the greens.

CLEAN BITES

- Must try cocktail: the 'In the Tall Grass'—crisp cucumer with vodka and apple, topped with champagne, grapefruit essence and riesling.
- Narcissa sources its produce and dairy from Balazs' The Farm at Locusts on Hudson. In fact, vegetables and herbs are planted specifically to support chef John Fraser's menu.

Cuisine:
American
(Contemporary)

Neighborhood:
Soho

Meals Served:
Brunch, Lunch,
Dinner

NAVY

137 Sullivan St.   navynyc.com
212-533-1137

Chef Camille Becerra is a supremely talented cook and food stylist. At the age of 19, Becerra studied macrobiotic cuisine and cooking at a Zen monastery, and it's clear that plenty of those ideas about conscious cooking weave their way into this stylish spot.

At Navy, you can inhabit her beautiful world and get a taste of it, too.

The 51-seat bar and restaurant is a cozy joint where neighbors stop by for coffee in the morning and dinner patrons spill out onto the tree-lined Soho street.

The space is designed with a maritime aesthetic, and you should take that as a clue to dive headfirst into anything on the menu that comes from the sea. Local oysters, clams, house-cured fish and sea urchin are found in abundance in smart preparations.

After seafood, the focus here is all vegetable love like the smoky charred cabbage that comes laced with a spice yogurt subtly sweetened with sweet potato and currants.

CLEAN BITES

- Becerra works closely with the Lancaster Farm Fresh Co-op to source her produce.
- Navy cures its fish in-house and makes its own caviar and crackers.
- Coffee is made with Brazilian beans from Kitten Coffee, a Brooklyn roaster.

NAYA EXPRESS

Multiple locations

nayarestaurants.com
@NayaExpress

NAYA
1057 2nd Ave
212-319-7777

Cuisine:
Middle Eastern

Neighborhood:
Multiple locations
(Express), Midtown
East

Meals Served:
Lunch, Dinner

The tomatoes at Lebanese spot Naya Express taste like tomatoes. The arugula tastes deliciously bitter, and the finely chopped flat leaf parsley, generously doused on, well, everything, has that characteristically crackley texture. This is fast food done right.

The kitchen produces shawarma, chicken taouk, beef kebabs, falafel—all delivered in a whole-wheat or white pita wrap or served on a vermicelli-adorned rice or salad bowl. Everything is finished with whatever toppings and sauces you point to (pickled turnips, garlic whip, tahini, spicy red sauce and jalapeno are among the myriad house-made options). The lines at Naya Express are long, but the staff moves quickly so don't be discouraged—just plan accordingly.

Naya serves higher-end Lebanese fare in a serene contemporary setting. Start your meal with a selection of mezze, which includes muhammara, a sweet and nutty red pepper dip, as well as the usual hummus, tabbouleh and baba ganoush. Try the incredibly flavorful grilled lamb chops with a spinach salad with onion, tomato, walnuts and a pomegranate-citrus dressing. Those on a date, be aware, the chef is not afraid to use garlic and za'atar (a blend of Middle Eastern herbs and spices).

CLEAN BITES

- Must try: At Naya Express, go for a variety of the cold appetizers. They are out of this world.
- They serve antibiotic- and hormone- free shawarma—a real rarity.

NORTHERN SPY FOOD CO.

Cuisine:
American
(Contemporary)

Neighborhood:
East Village

Meals Served:
Brunch, Lunch, Dinner

511 E. 12th St.
212-228-5100

northernspyfoodco.com
@northernspyfood

$$$

Named after one of New York's oldest heirloom apples, Northern Spy Food Co. is an eatery built on fine cooking, sustainably raised meats, whole grains and loads of charm.

The smallish menu champions ingredients produced by regional farmers and artisan purveyors. The kitchen receives full sides of organic Fleisher's pork weekly and transforms them into brined and grilled loin steaks, roasted aromatic porchettas and succulent pork terrines.

It's hard to choose among the unique snacks and sides on the menu—think pickled eggs, peach gazpacho and a kale salad that is often credited with starting the city-wide craze. Everything on the menu feels light; especially dishes like ricotta, pita and gooseberry compote. The dishes are satisfying and thoughtful and often feature unique touches. For example, the addition of fava beans on trout with spring onions and sofrito added a nice earthiness.

With such charismatic food and an utterly alluring venue, if we lived in the East Village, we would want to make Northern Spy's cerulean-blue banquettes our second home.

CLEAN BITES

- Must try: brunch. With dishes like kale hash with poached eggs, the lively brunch is a particular highlight here.
- The tabletops are repurposed wooden bowling alley lanes.
- The restaurant has a Snail of Approval from Slow Food NYC.

ORGANIC AVENUE

Multiple locations   organicavenue.com
                      @organicavenue

Cuisine:
Vegetarian/Vegan

Meals Served:
Breakfast, Lunch,
Dinner

The leaders of the cold-pressed juice craze in NYC are now spearheading the trend of 100% organic, plant-based fast food. In addition to Organic Avenue's traditional juices, smoothies, raw foods and elixirs, it now offers a variety of soups, sides, rice and quinoa bowls, salads, and wraps—all ready to grab-and-go.

The options are extensive, and while from a nutritional standpoint we recommend choosing the collard green wraps, we must admit we really dug the falafel whole-wheat wrap made with sunflower falafel, hummus, tzatziki and smoked paprika.

We also liked the smoothie bowls, a take on the über-popular açai bowl trend in Los Angeles. Think smoothie poured over granola, topped with fresh fruit served in a bowl and enjoyed via spoon.

Our absolute favorite was the kale quinoa salad. The currants added a punch of sweetness, while the cashew dressing was rich and creamy even though it contained no dairy.

With ample choices of food you can feel good about eating, and locations in Midtown Manhattan, a visit to Organic Avenue is the perfect way to show off your healthy eating habits back at the office.

CLEAN BITES

- Check out their 'Feed Your Brain' blog with recipes for plant-based popsicles and healthy lifestyle tips.
- Heads up: Some of Organic Avenue's locations have more limited menu options than others.

Cuisine:
Italian, Latin American,
Mediterranean

Neighborhood:
West Village

Meals Served:
Brunch, Lunch, Dinner

ORGANIKA

89 7th Ave. S.
212-414-1900

organikanyc.com
@OrganikaNYC

What do you call a polished, all-organic eatery? Why, Organika, of course. This Italian-leaning spot offers organic wines with simple Mediterranean fare.

The menu is broken down into antipasti, bruschetta, salads, pizzas and pastas, with a daily roster of entrées inspired by the season. Many options are veggie-friendly and a few are vegan-able—though not intending to be. The plentiful salads are full of crisp produce and could easily stand in for an entrée. The pizza is passable, but it is the pasta that solicited low, happy moans from our table. The seared tuna seasoned with pink pepper and mint has a light fresh flavor, which juxtaposes the side of warm mashed sweet potatoes we indulged in.

All the ingredients on the menu are organic, local, or imported from artisanal producers (like the golden Umbrian olive oil that lines the counter). And just in case you doubt the origin of the capers, you can double-check their qualifications on the Food Product Origin card on the back of the menu.

CLEAN BITES

- All of the wines, beers and cocktails here are 100% organic.
- All food is used within 48 hours of delivery.
- Organika offers live music most Tuesdays.

ORGANIQUE

110 E. 23rd St.
212-674-2229

organiqueonline.com

Cuisine:
American (Casual)

Neighborhood:
Gramercy Park

Meals Served:
Breakfast, Lunch,
Dinner

Of the multitude of Midtown delis, it's pretty swell to find one that offers clean, organic produce and meats for only a dollar or two more. This slim space is set up like a typical New York deli, with a handful of white plastic tables and a few chairs lining the walls, but the similarities stop there.

Of the all-organic meats, we liked the turkey and the wild salmon flecked with dill. (Get there on the early side of the lunch rush—the fish tends to dry out on the heated buffet tins.)

Take advantage of the salad bar, with dressings like agave-sweetened miso, or some of the delicious roast vegetable options. Deep-orange sweet potatoes came dotted with plump cranberries, and a twist on ratatouille, a mélange of roast eggplant and tomatoes, was melt-in-your-mouth tasty.

CLEAN BITES

- Organique is a fine place to pick up lunch to-go, or an organic cup of joe in the morning.
- The restaurant offers gluten-free, whole-grain bread to help you create your own sandwich.

Cuisine:
Latin American,
Carribean

Neighborhood:
Park Slope

Meals Served:
Brunch, Dinner

PALO SANTO

652 Union St.
718-636-6311

palosantorestaurant.com
@PaloSantoPS

Before any of Jacques Gautier's Latin American market cooking hits your lips, simply mouthing words from his menu is delicious: Asopado de Mariscos. Cazuela de Hongos.

Palo Santo occupies the ground floor of a brownstone in Park Slope, where the menu changes daily. Mellow Caribbean music, exposed brick walls and a garden where fresh herbs grow wild complete the down-to-earth vibe.

There is something lighthearted about Gautier's cuisine, both in presentation and flavor. Lamb tacos are hard to resist when you learn every tortilla is made to order. Pan roasted bluefish topped with salsa verde arrived on a bright green stripe of banana leaf. A superlative grass-fed ribeye comes artfully topped with grilled onions.

At Palo Santo there are no precise rules or recipes—only passionate cooking from the heart.

CLEAN BITES

- Must try: coconut plantain stew.
- Palo Santo's rooftop is home to a small-scale urban farm where vegetables are grown and organic waste is composted. Fresh herbs and evergreens grow in the small back garden where customers dine when the weather is warm.
- Paintings by local artists adorn the walls here, demonstrating that Palo Santo really is a community hub.

PEACEFOOD CAFE

41 E. 11th St.
212-979-2288

peacefoodcafe.com
@peacefoodnyc

460 Amsterdam Ave.
212-362-2266

Cuisine:
Vegetarian/Vegan

Neighborhood:
Union Square, Upper
West Side

Meals Served:
Breakfast, Lunch,
Dinner

The two locations of this casual cafe serve up gourmet vegan food and delectable pastries. Salads, soups, sandwiches and pizzas are full of creative twists and bright flavors, and happily they don't rely on mock meat or deep frying.

Appetizers like Shanghai-style dumplings filled with chives and mushrooms and vegetable tamales are perfect to share. Chickpea fries release a molten wave of creamy, herb-flecked puree when you bite into the crisp crust. The Asian salad is especially good—a heaping pile of greens, baby Asian vegetables, sprouts and baked tempeh with sesame vinaigrette.

Save space for dessert: There is a dizzying array of options, including spelt-based, gluten-free and vegan treats. A few options are even sweetened with maple syrup. Don't pass up the raw keylime pie— it's so tangy and rich you won't believe it's vegan.

CLEAN BITES

- Load up on antioxidants with Peacefood's array of smoothie and juice options.
- Trying to add more raw foods to your diet? A section of Peacefood's menu is dedicated to raw-food offerings and is fully kosher.
- Online ordering is available.

Cuisine:
American (Casual),
British

Meals Served:
Breakfast, Lunch,
Dinner

PRET A MANGER

Multiple locations

pret.com
@Pret

This simple, organic and locally focused chain is an English import, and it ably contradicts any lingering misapprehensions about the caliber of that country's food.

The charming shops proffer sandwiches, soups, cakes, cookies, muffins, juice and coffees, and the myriad locations across the city are usually packed with Gothamites. Try the slim, tea-style sandwich stuffed with plush avocado and organic Bell & Evans chicken, or one of the salads—we especially enjoyed one with lobster and yellow peppers.

Pret, as the locals call it, also succeeds in the beverage arena: The fair-trade, organic coffee is very good, and the beans are rotated (and composted) every two weeks. The organic milk offered alongside is a swell bonus.

The fact that most food containers are as biodegradable as possible will make most diners feel even better about their meal as they dash back to work.

CLEAN BITES

- Everything here is made fresh daily (a rarity for a grab-and-go chain), and leftover sandwiches are donated to charity.
- Many locations have free Wi-Fi.

PRINT

653 11th Ave.
212-757-2224

printrestaurant.com
@printrestaurant

Cuisine:
American
(Contemporary)

Neighborhood:
Hell's Kitchen

Meals Served:
Breakfast, Brunch,
Lunch, Dinner

$$$

The only reasonable explanation for Print's under-the-radar status is its far west location. The farm-to-table restaurant, located in the Ink48 Hotel, may be a harrowing hike from the subway, but the menu's goat cheese gnocchi alone is worth the walk. The dish's rich, salty ingredients (crispy pancetta and the puffy, cheese-laden capsules) as well as its nutritious produce (squash blossoms, summer squash and shell peas) create a balanced mix of winter comfort food and lighter, refreshing summer fare.

The cauliflower lemon soup is also reason enough to head to 11th Avenue. Among the summer's boon of chilled purees and gazpachos, this warm, creamy response is a true standout.

Print's entrées effectively integrate local, organic veggie sides and humanely raised proteins (just check the website to see a list of the restaurant's purveyours). Exhibit A: the duck, with its flavorful jus melding with translucent kohlrabi rectangles and a bed of greens with juicy red berries. Similarly, a red snapper dish creatively invokes the flavors of a fresh bowl of New England clam chowder.

CLEAN BITES

- Check out the rooftop lounge, Press, for cocktails and unobstructed views of Manhattan and the Hudson. (The restaurant also has a garden on the rooftop!)
- Print employs a full-time forager to source local ingredients.
- Print participates in many community development projects, including volunteering with programs such as Wellness in the Schools, Slow Food NYC and Just Food.

Cuisine:
Italian

Neighborhood:
Noho

Meals Served:
Lunch, Dinner

QUARTINO BOTTEGA ORGANICA

11 Bleecker St. quartino.com
212-529-5133 @QuartinoNYC

Many of us are under the impression that whole-wheat pasta is always going to be second best. Not so at Quartino Bottega Organica, where whole-wheat pasta really shines in the fairytale-esque garden. Here, organic pasta is made on the premises and served with meltingly tender baby artichoke hearts and a dusting of Parmigiano Reggiano.

Pescatarians take heed: There's no beef or chicken here, but there is always a fish of the day, simply treated (usually grilled or baked). The menu is trim but well-curated: vegan options, focaccia, whole-wheat pizza and veggie sides such as excellent baked spinach.

Wine drinkers should know that there are plenty of organic vinos available. With an interior decked out with copper accents and pretty, dimmed lights, Quartino Bottega Organica would be an ideal date spot, in or out of the garden.

CLEAN BITES

- All of the organic extra-virgin olive oil used is made from same-day cold-pressed olives harvested at Quartino's Ligurian family farm in Italy.
- The kitchen cleans with organic vegetable-derived soaps and does not use any plastic items.
- All desserts are 100% organic.
- At the end of the evening, Quartino donates unsold organic whole-wheat bread to the Bowery Mission shelter.

REYNARD

80 Wythe Ave. reynardnyc.com
718-460-8004

Cuisine:
American
(Contemporary)

Neighborhood:
Williamsburg

Meals Served:
Breakfast, Brunch,
Lunch, Dinner

A reservation at Reynard, in the Wythe Hotel, on a
Saturday night is your golden ticket (found in a Mast Brothers chocolate
bar, of course) past the street-long line of artsy 20-somethings waiting
for a spot at the rooftop bar.

While the crowd screams millennials, the space has a long history.
The building was originally a textile factory in the early 1900s, and
although it has been refurbished, some of the original building
materials are still intact.

Reynard's menu changes daily and features masterfully prepared,
thoughtfully procured ingredients, proving its food production is
anything but factory-like.

The grilled quail was a standout, served whole with kale, cherries,
proscuitto and rich truffle butter. It was tender and satisfying. And
there are always seasonal veggie options.

End your meal with a nutty tang of carrot cake and macademia
nut ice cream.

CLEAN BITES

- Reynard also has a more permanent, all-day menu featuring a grass-fed burger with caramelized onion and gruyere that we could eat all day long.
- Small plates are now available at The Ides (the rooftop bar) as well.

Cuisine:
American
(Contemporary)

Neighborhood:
Kips Bay

Meals Served:
Brunch, Lunch, Dinner

RIVERPARK

450 E. 29th St.
212-729-9790

riverparknyc.com
@RiverparkNYC

While many Manhattan restaurants resort to sourcing produce from area farms or greenmarkets, Riverpark takes the farm-to-table concept to another level. Tom Colicchio's waterfront eatery churns out seasonal specialties boasting ingredients directly from an expansive on-site farm.

If the weather is on your side, settle into the spacious and sleek outdoor terrace overlooking the East River.

Chef Bryan Hunt mans the kitchen, producing oft-changing menus of internally influenced American dishes. If they're available, don't miss the buffalo's milk burrata enhanced with heirloom tomatoes, apricots, peaches and basil. Locally caught seafood and hormone- and antibiotic-free meats are showcased as entrées. The Mediterranean-style lamb burger is a standout: tender meat layered with sharp pecorino, kale slaw and roasted tomato on a toasted English muffin alongside garlicky fries and tzatziki.

With water views, fresh fare and the award-winning Riverpark Farm, this lush green oasis offers a touch of solace from city life.

CLEAN BITES

- Must try: sweet-corn panna cotta with peekytoe crab salad, avocado and cilantro.
- Stop in anytime. A limited menu is available to guests between lunch/brunch and dinner services.
- Check out riverparkfarm.com for more info on Riverpark's farm and to join one of the regularly scheduled tours or workshops.

ROMAN'S

243 Dekalb Ave.   romansnyc.com
718-622-5300

Cuisine:
Italian

Neighborhood:
Fort Greene

Meals Served:
Lunch, Dinner

The white-tiled walls and marble-topped bar here match the simplicity of the ever-changing graph-paper menu at this little Fort Greene Italian trattoria. Don't count on returning for your favorite dish, but bank on discovering a new favorite with each visit.

The menu begs to be indulged through (at least) three courses. Follow thick slices of fresh bread with a starter like fava beans and pesto. The creamy beans are the perfect when combined with the herbiness of the pesto. Pasta like anelli spiked with sausage, eggplant and ricotta always beckons.

We are fans of the classic Roman cavatelli with chickpeas and peppers that delivers an Italian freshness we can't resist.

With a few white-clothed tables tucked away from crowded communal tables and regulars at the bar, Roman's effortless vibe may deceive you; food this good doesn't come easy.

CLEAN BITES

- Roman's is brought to you by the Diner (p. 98), Marlow & Sons (p. 128), and Reynard (p. 147) gang.
- If you love that thick bread, you can take some home. Roman's makes and sells its own sourdough bread under the name She Wolf Bakery, and it's made with organic grains and a traditional sourdough culture that makes it easier on the digestive system.

Cuisine:
Italian

Neighborhood:
Greenwich Village

Meals Served:
Breakfast, Brunch,
Lunch, Dinner

ROSEMARY'S

18 Greenwich Ave.
212-647-1818

rosemarysnyc.com
@Rosemarysnyc

$$$

Rosemary's Enoteca & Trattoria's al fresco feel makes the crowds—who pack the place from door to bar even on a Monday—bearable.

The classic Italian fare is spun from local ingredients (some from Rosemary's own rooftop farm!) and the plates beg to be shared.

Verdure, like chili-spiced cabbage with pecorino and almonds, eggplant caponata with balsamic, olives and capers, pack flavor into charming little ramekins. The frutti di mare includes a refreshing ginger, lemon, jalapeno and mint shrimp. A chopped salad is a motley mix of escarole, sliced artichoke, olives, raisins, caper berries, cherry tomatoes, chickpeas, ricotta salata and sunflower seeds.

Dive into homemade pastas, like perfectly cooked orecchiette with braised greens and tasty crumbles of homemade sausage.

As long as Rosemary's keeps bringing the food from rooftop to table, the crowds will keep coming.

CLEAN BITES

- Rosemary's has a live rooftop webcam, where you can literally watch grass (and produce) grow.
- Rosemary's partners with community gardens that help educate the community on the importance of urban sustainability programming.

ROSIE'S

29 E. 2nd St.
212-335-0114

rosiesnyc.com
@Rosiesnyc

Cuisine:
Mexican

Neighborhood:
East Village

Meals Served:
Brunch, Lunch, Dinner

$$ \$\$ $$

Located on a lively East Village corner, Rosie's serves up a thoughtful approach to the bold, complex flavors of Mexico.

In the kitchen, chefs Angel Andrade and Chester Gerl Meyer prepare straightforward, brightly flavored dishes made using traditional techniques. This means they take the time to grind fresh masa for tortillas and cook on a traditional comal (a flat griddle) located in the middle of the 90-seat dining room, which was designed to resemble an open-air market.

The menu focuses on the many varied regional cuisines of Mexico, prepared with market-fresh ingredients. An orange- and chile-rubbed whole local porgy comes with chipotle-lime mayo, charred spring onions and a bundle of tortillas on the side. Add an order of quelites, sautéed Mexican wild greens, for an extra vegetable punch.

The restaurant is tuned into special diets, without kowtowing to them. Many options are vegetarian, only three entrees have gluten and all is flavorful without smothering everything in sight with cheese.

CLEAN BITES

- Before you waltz out the door, pick up a temporary Rosie's tattoo from the hostess stand to wear your love for the place, literally, on your sleeve.
- If you love Rosie's, try Marc Meyer's other spots, Cookshop (p.92), Hundred Acres (p. 116) and Vic's (p.163)—all Clean Plates-approved dining destinations.

Cuisine:
Italian

Neighborhood:
Boerum Hill

Meals Served:
Breakfast, Brunch,
Lunch, Dinner

RUCOLA

190 Dean St.
718-576-3209

rucolabrooklyn.com
@rucolanyc

Every step nearer confirms your original instinct: You've discovered something special.

Tucked in a corner of Boreum Hill's Historic District, Rucola is one of Brooklyn's more gorgeous takes on rustic farmhouse design. Light flickers from milk-bottle-on-wheel chandeliers, and tea candles set on stacked wooden crates gently illuminate the weathered space.

Rucola executes a simple concept well: fresh, local, seasonal northern Italian dining. This is clear from the first bite—a salad of the restaurant's namesake bitter green with shaved radish and Parmesan featured a light but complex celery seed vinaigrette. Brilliant green swiss chard clings to al dente twists of pasta with grana Padano and oregano in the spaghetti. A Long Island duck, served wonderfully rare, comes with a perfect garnish of bing cherries, tarragon and roasted fennel resting on red quinoa.

It's easy to see why so many Boerum Hill denizens are crazy about this place and why non-neighbors wish it was in their 'hood.

CLEAN BITES

- Must try: the delectable antipasti selection, with vegetarian options.
- Rucola's cooking techniques are inspired by the slow food movement in Piedmont, Italy.

SACRED CHOW

227 Sullivan St. sacredchow.com
212-337-0863 @sacredchow

Cuisine:
Vegetarian/Vegan

Neighborhood:
Greenwich Village

Meals Served:
Brunch, Lunch, Dinner

Northwest-born New Yorkers will saunter through the door of this little vegan cafe and do a double-take: It's a dead ringer for any Portland, Oregon cafe.

The hippie vibe is on the premises in a major way. Gargantuan faux-Japanese lanterns dangle overhead, and cynical Gothamites will have to bite their tongues at the sincerity of it all. But the delicious, 95% organic food and superlative brunch will get them talking again.

The big scramble tofu bowl (so egg-like it might make you experience momentary disorientation) is served with a side of steamed broccoli and roasted beets. Belgian waffles wow with their plushness, covered with cinnamon apple compote and coconut whipped cream.

Those with dietary restrictions will be pleased to see that the menu identifies dishes prepared without gluten, wheat, soy or sugar, so they can order without having to question the waiter.

CLEAN BITES

- The restaurant is certified kosher.
- Sacred Chow runs a daily special of soup and bread for just $10.

Cuisine:
Indian

Neighborhood:
Greenwich Village

Meals Served:
Lunch, Dinner

SOHO TIFFIN JUNCTION

42 E. 8th St.   sohotiffin.com
917-514-8409   @sohotiffin

Just north of Washington Square, NYU students, Indian expats and pleasure-seeking vegans congregate in this sleek, wood-and-metal storefront in search of heart-healthy Indian food.

"Tiffin," British-Indian slang for a light meal, usually refers to a packed lunch carried to work or school in a multi-tiered metal lunchbox. The owners drew inspiration from the Chipotle empire, which pioneered the concept of fresh, organic, cafeteria-style fast food, but have replaced Tex-Mex with Indian fusion. Patrons select from a range of fillings and toppings as they move through the line, starting with a protein (like pulled pork, egg white, or kale), then adding rice gently spiced with lemon and curry leaf and a variety of sauces, chutneys, and pickles. The only fried items on the menu are the dosas—sourdough crepes—and plantain chips. Even the kale chips are baked.

CLEAN BITES

- Must try: shredded beef braised in a mild mangalorean (coconut-ginger-garlic) sauce, served in a dosa and topped with spicy tomato-chili sauce.
- The restaurant uses rice bran oil for frying instead of other GMO-infested fats.
- Every item on Soho Tiffin Junction's menu is gluten-and-soy free.

SOUEN

Multiple locations   souen.net
@SouenNoodle

Cuisine:
Asian, Macrobiotic

Meals Served:
Lunch, Dinner

Stepping into Souen is like discovering a tiny slice of California on a teeming NYC street.

Everything here is organic, dark greens are plentiful and desserts are naturally sweetened. Even diners who flip when they see the word "macrobiotic" will remain calm here: Seafood and sushi options are abundant, so there truly is something for everyone.

The absence of refined sugar—and even salt—becomes a comfort when digging into the clean-tasting food. Try steamed greens with a creamy carrot dressing, and a steamed shrimp roll bundled in nori with watercress, avocado, cucumbers and burdock.

Desserts, like the chocolate parfait and the fruit kanten, have no sugar, egg, dairy or wheat. Instead, they are sweetened with maple syrup. With seaweed, piles of veggies, and no sugar in sight, Souen is a champion in the realm of health.

CLEAN BITES

- Must try: cold-pressed seasonal juices like watermelon with pineapple and mint.
- The tofu is organic.
- Want to learn more about macrobiotics? Check out the restaurant's website to learn more about the abundance of healthful, traditional macrobiotic foods Souen offers.

Cuisine:
American
(Contemporary)

Neighborhood:
Upper West Side, Soho

Meals Served:
Breakfast (Spring
Street), Brunch, Lunch,
Dinner

SPRING NATURAL KITCHEN

474 Columbus Ave.   springnaturalkitchen.com
646-596-7434

SPRING STREET NATURAL

62 Spring St.   springstreetnatural.com
212-966-0290   @springstnatural

The open and airy Spring Natural Kitchen serves seasonal foods with vegan and vegetarian options alongside grass-fed, free-range meat. The conscious and extensive menu also features clearly labeled gluten-free dishes.

Tuck into a Korean marinated hanger steak that is slathered in shiro miso-sesame sauce. A fresh apricot salad features red and golden quinoa, avocado, zucchini, toasted almonds and a ginger dressing. The roasted organic salmon is refreshingly vibrant on a bed of jasmine rice along with grilled Japanese eggplant and watercress salad.

Down in Soho, the soaring windows of sister spot Spring Street Natural let the sun shine in. Tasty good-for-you foods can be found here, including organic eggs, garlicky spinach spritzed with lemon, many organic meats and a tower of tempeh for the snack-craving vegan. We like it for a midday fix of American cuisine with vegan and vegetarian options.

CLEAN BITES

- Whenever possible, pie crusts, breads, pastas and sausages are made in-house.

THE STANDARD GRILL

848 Washington St.
212-645-4100

thestandardgrill.com
@StandardGrill

Cuisine:
American
(Contemporary)

Neighborhood:
Meatpacking District

Meals Served:
Breakfast, Brunch,
Lunch, Dinner

Tucked under the West Side's High Line, the flagship restaurant of André Balazs' Standard Hotel is a novel addition to the trendy Meatpacking District. In a neighborhood renowned for a bevy of pretentious hotspots, The Standard Grill is a welcome find with its sophisticated, laid-back atmosphere and exceptionally friendly service.

With a heavy emphasis on market-fresh ingredients, chef Ron Rosselli presents a seasonal menu of refined and updated classic American fare. A silken chilled pea soup with a cool whipped coconut milk with crunchy almonds and snap peas is a true appetizer knockout. Entrées are elegantly presented, including an Atlantic salmon over rustic rye berries, pickled turnips enlivened with a poppy seed dressing. Pick from vegetable accompaniments like bok choy with bits of Ibérico ham and pickled ramps.

Overall, with an inviting ambiance, attentive staff and inspired cuisine, one thing is certain: There's nothing standard about this grill.

CLEAN BITES

- If you are taking out-of-town-visitors to walk the High Line, this is the perfect place for a bite after a stroll.
- The restaurant offers a large selection of oysters—get your zinc on!
- Look closely at the floor: It's embedded with thousands of copper pennies.

Cuisine:
Vegetarian/Vegan

Neighborhood: Park
Slope, Tribeca

Meals Served:
Breakfast, Brunch,
Lunch, Dinner

SUN IN BLOOM

460 Bergen St.
718-622-4303

suninbloom.com
@SunInBloom

165 Church St.
212-791-6700

Light pervades Sun In Bloom, from its soothing setting to its invigorating cuisine.

SIB's food is proudly holistic: 100% organic, gluten-free, vegan, kosher and either raw or raw-optional.

Liquid remedies run the gamut from pressed Norwalk juices to nut mylks and smoothies. Vinegar adds a touch of tart to the açai-crunch smoothie, a delicious puree of soy mylk, berries, banana and live granola.

Try the cool, purifying, raw alkalizing soup, which includes cucumber, avocado, parsley, romaine, garlic, lemon, salt, olive oil and kangen (alkalizing) water with a collard green wrap on the side.

The Bella Divine salad, is just that—divine—and features kale massaged in a sesame ginger dressing with creamy avocado, sunflower sprouts and sauerkraut, finished with dulse and caraway seeds.

It doesn't get much cleaner than this.

CLEAN BITES

- While the Park Slope restaurant is full-service, the Tribeca location is set up as a counter-service cafe with grab-and-go takeaway.
- Sun In Bloom offers three- or five-day organic juice cleanses, tailored to specific needs.
- Need kosher or raw food? Sun In Bloom has you covered.

SWEETGREEN

Multiple locations   sweetgreen.com
                             @sweetgreen

Cuisine:
American (Casual)

Meals Served:
Lunch, Dinner

Manhattan has embraced this fast-casual D.C.-based salad chain with open arms, and for good reason. Sweetgreen focuses on sustainably sourced, organic ingredients from area farmers and purveyors.

Customers can design made-to-order salads and wrap masterpieces with a base of options—warm quinoa and farro grains; shredded kale, chopped romaine, organic mesclun, arugula, and baby spinach—and an array of proteins, including vegetarian options like baked falafel. You can even scatter add-ons like assorted veggies, fruits, nuts and organic seeds on top. Or, simply choose from several featured combos like the hearty "guacamole greens" with tender roasted chicken, creamy avocado, grape tomatoes, red onion and crushed tortilla chips, topped with a lime-cilantro-jalapeno vinaigrette and fresh lime juice.

Both locations offer an organic frozen yogurt bar, Sweetflow, but the location adjacent to the NoMad Hotel (in Flatiron) also offers organic, cold-pressed juices called Sweetpress.

CLEAN BITES

- Sweetgreen vendors are proudly displayed.
- Sweetgreen is on it when it comes to both eating and building green: The furniture is made from reclaimed wood, the paint is low-VOC, the kitchen composts, and bowls, cutlery and beverage cups are all 100% plant-based compostable packaging not derived from oil.

TELEPAN

72 W. 69th St.
212-580-4300

telepan-ny.com
@billtelepan

Cuisine:
American
(Contemporary)

Neighborhood:
Upper West Side

Meals Served:
Brunch, Lunch, Dinner

Choose your ambiance at relaxed-yet-refined Telepan. Impressing a date? Opt to sit in the cozy brown leather banquettes. Business lunch? Head towards the larger four-top tables.

Telepan takes the root of its food seriously, the Euro-flecked fare made from sparklingly fresh produce, and organic meat sourced within 250 miles whenever possible. Chef-owner Bill Telepan has worked with such Gallic luminaries as Daniel Boulud and Gilbert Le Coze, and it shows, both in a classic cheese gougères amuse-bouche paired with bright, flavorful gazpacho and a hanger steak glazed in decadent oxtail bone-marrow sauce.

CLEAN BITES

- Must try: zucchini and egg pasta.
- Make sure to check out Telepan's contemporary art, most of it featuring lush images of produce.
- Bill Telepan stays busy. He is also executive chef of Wellness in the Schools (WITS), a nonprofit organization dedicated to making school food healthy.

UNTITLED

99 Gansevoort St.
212-570-3670

untitledatthewhitney.com
@untitlednyc

Cuisine:
American
(Contemporary), Small
Plates

Neighborhood:
Meatpacking District

Meals Served:
Lunch, Dinner

There's a delicious installation at The Whitney Museum of American Art. And it's a permanent one: At the museum's restaurant, Untitled, you can eat everything in sight.

The Renzo Piano-designed restaurant, punctuated with poppy red chairs, got the same careful consideration that the galleries do.

While we don't pretend to understand all of the art upstairs, we do know that chef Michael Anthony is clearly a master artist when it comes to creating dishes like pole beans with calamari and hazelnuts and turnips with string beans, guanciale and pecorino.

The menu has a fun mix-and-match feel that is free of defined categories. While the larger main courses (featuring sustainably sourced fish and antibiotic- and hormone-free meats) sounded lovely, we found ourselves ordering mostly from the small plates, which are based around vegetables and make up the "meat" of the menu, like beets with yogurt and summery lemon verbena.

CLEAN BITES

- The restaurant, located at the base of the High Line, makes for a great stop post-stroll.
- Untitled composts all of food scraps, recycles all of spent oil, glass, plastic and paper products.
- Take a look at what the butter is served on when it accompanies bread to the table— it's the same tile used for the flooring!

Cuisine:
Italian, Californian

Neighborhood:
Gramercy

Meals Served:
Brunch, Lunch, Dinner

UPLAND

345 Park Ave. S.
211-686-1006

uplandnyc.com
@upland_nyc

$$$

Feeling frustrated at your lack of ability to cross space and time borders? Head to Upland: it's like visiting California and Italy all at once.

This Gramercy restaurant from Justin Smillie is a beacon of bright citrus, California cool and Italian warmth.

Interesting vegetable preparations abound. There is the hunk of maitake mushrooms, crisped in olive oil and resting on a bed of tangy farmstead cheese, beets with white chocolate and slow-roasted celery root with black truffle butter.

We loved that every dish we tried highlighted vegetables—and none of which were overcooked or hidden under heavy sauces. Take the porcelet from Flying Pig Farms: this crackling piece of pork is ringed with slender, sweet heirloom Jimmy Nardello peppers, charred onions and pieces of persimmon.

Upland can't change the weather outside, but it can give you the warm fuzzies with its food, technique and welcoming atmosphere (all queries about food or ingredient-sourcing are welcome here).

CLEAN BITES

- Smillie previously worked at Il Buco Alimentari & Vineria (p. 117), another Clean Plates favorite.
- The restaurant is named for the small California town Smillie was born in.

VIC'S

31 Great Jones St.
212-253-5700

vicsnewyork.com
@vicsnewyork

Cuisine:
American Italian,
Mediterranean

Neighborhood:
NoHo

Meals Served:
Brunch, Dinner

With its copper bar, massive skylight and exposed-brick walls, this NoHo revamp of the neighborhood favorite Five Points is easy to settle into.

Vic's is the kind of place that makes us smack our heads and go "why can't more restaurants be like this?", where it's possible to go nuts ordering one night (pork shoulder with pink peppercorns) and keep things more healthful the next (poached cod with kale, Meyer lemon, leeks and almonds).

We'd happily eat a meal composed of chef Hillary Sterling's rollicking seasonal vegetables (no boring sides here). Roasted squash is jazzed up with brown butter vinaigrette and balsamic-almond bread crumbs, while heirloom carrots are radiant when dashed with dill, capers and roasted shallots. Vegetables even wend their way into dessert: Look for parsnips in the honey cake.

It's the little touches here that happily threatens to turns us all into regulars, including kicky goat butter, the availability of half-size portions of every pasta dish and simple belly warmers like a fennel-tomato broth minestrone with kale and parsnips.

CLEAN BITES

- Fun factoid: Back in the day, the location was the Astor family's stables.

Cuisine:
American
(Contemporary)

Neighborhood:
Vinegar Hill

Meals Served:
Brunch, Dinner

VINEGAR HILL HOUSE

72 Hudson Ave.   vinegarhillhouse.com
718-522-1018   @vinhillhouse

Replete with mismatched vintage flatware, chipped walls and a tumbleweed chandelier, Vinegar Hill House is an archetypically haute-barnyard neighborhood spot. Yet those who crowd around the tables and spill onto the sidewalk clearly hail from beyond Vinegar Hill's three-block radius.

The food, much of it prepared in the restaurant's cramped kitchen with a wood-burning stove, is deserving of both hype and wait.

Vinegar Hill House's signature dish is a cast iron chicken, but the pork and grits are its masterpiece. A cut above all other hogs, the Red Wattle pork's charred skin gives way to a pink center that is tender and almost beef-like. Vegetarians must try the charred beets where all of the beet is used including the greens in a pistou combined with saffron yogurt and pistachios.

If you haven't yet found your way here yet, superlative seasonal food in one of the quaintest spots (and on one of the quaintest blocks) in Brooklyn should be incentive enough to put it on your map.

CLEAN BITES

- Brunch must try: sourdough strawberry pancake.
- When the weather is nice, try to sit in the quiet garden, under a cherry tree.

WASSAIL

162 Orchard St.
646-918-6835

wassailnyc.com
@WassailNYC

Cuisine:
American
(Contemporary),
Vegetarian, Small
Plates

Neighborhood:
Lower East Side

Meals Served:
Brunch, Dinner

The best part about Wassail's vegetarian status? It's not a thing; it just is. The fact that the menu is vegetarian is just one of many excellent reasons to visit this Lower East Side spot.

There is a friendly community vibe here along with a serious focus on local sourcing, foraging and composting leftovers through Reclaimed Organics. There's also a party-up-front, business-in-the-back situation going on with a lively bar scene in the fore, and a restaurant holding it down in the aft.

Chef Joseph Buenconsejo's modern cuisine plays up vegetables and grains and plays off Wassail's incredible selection of fermented hard cider. Of the 12 ciders on draft, more than half are locally made.

While the cider program is innovative and the cuisine is bright and inventive, it's pastry chef Rebecca Eichenbaum's vegetable-driven desserts that really left our heads spinning.

Her vegetal desserts combine leaves, blossoms, stems and roots and atypical ingredients like knotweed, buckwheat and sorrel for surprising and delicious results.

CLEAN BITES

- Husband-and-wife team Jennifer Lim and Ben Sandler also own the excellent The Queens Kickshaw (p. 171) in Astoria.
- Wassail offers a private dining room with room for up to 22 people.

Cuisine:
Mexican

Neighborhood:
Williamsburg

Meals Served:
Brunch, Dinner

ZONA ROSA

571 Lorimer St.
917-324-7423

zonarosabrooklyn.com
@ZonaRosaBkln

It's fitting that Zona Rosa, named after one of the hippest neighborhoods in Mexico City, has found a home in one of the hippest neighborhoods in NYC. True to its name, the fare is authentic Mexican, featuring tortas, enchiladas, mole, tacos and ceviche with no burritos or quesadillas in sight.

Chef Ivan Garcia (not surprisingly, an implant from Mexico City) nailed the guacamole—it was perfectly salted with chunks of avocado served with tortilla chips so fresh you could actually taste the corn. A starter salad—a nice portion of romaine, watermelon, cotija cheese and pumpkin seed—was refreshing on a summer evening. The tacos (choose among pork, beef, mahi mahi and Swiss chard, cheese and avocado) get extra points for arriving with three house-made hot sauces. Garcia's secret family mole recipe truly shined in the enmoladas.

Overall, the fare was solid, and because its meats are grass-fed, we'd choose Zona Rosa over other Mexican spots any time.

CLEAN BITES

- Must try: coconut churros with caramel.
- The kitchen is in a converted Airstream that faces towards the street.
- Zona Rosa is brought to you by the same creative team as Mesa Coyoacan (p.131).

BEYOND RESTAURANTS

BAKERIES

BABYCAKES
Gluten-free, soy-free, non-GMO and vegan cupcakes with veggie-based food dyes. Served by ladies clad in old-school diner themed uniforms.
248 Broome St. | Lower East Side | erinmckennasbakery.com

BIEN CUIT
Breads and pastries made with local flours, slow fermentation techniques and produce from local farms that will transport you straight to Paris.
120 Smith St. | Carroll Gardens | biencuit.com

BIRDBATH
Wind-powered bakery with some meals to-go. The breads and pastries made with organic and local ingredients. Brought to you by the City Bakery (p. 89) team.
Multiple locations | thecitybakery.com

BLOSSOM BAKERY
Vegan, organic and kosher bakery with ample gluten-free options. Serves pastries, cakes and pies. They also offer private classes. Brought to you by the Blossom (p. 79) team.
174 9th Ave. | Chelsea | blossombakerynyc.com

CLEMENTINE BAKERY
All-vegan and organic selection of baked goods, sandwiches and made-to-order cakes. Brews Kitten Coffee. Gluten-free options available.
229 Greene Ave. | Bedford-Stuyvesant | clementinebakery.com

FOUR AND TWENTY BLACKBIRDS

Pies made with locally sourced, seasonal ingredients and natural sweeteners that will put your mom's to shame. They serve Stumptown coffee.

Multiple locations | birdsblack.com

JENNIFER'S WAY

100% gluten-free facility serving soy-free baked goods with nutrient-rich grains and natural sweeteners. Oh, and they don't taste like cardboard.

263 E. 10th St. | East Village | jenniferswaybakery.com

PEACE FOOD BAKERY

Dairy, egg and refined sugar-free baked goods with raw and gluten-free options also available. Check out their full restaurant on p. 143.

Multiple locations | peacefoodcafe.com

TATZ GOURMET SWEETZ

Gluten-free, soy-free, refined sugar-free and mostly organic vegan desserts.

844 Amsterdam Ave. | Morningside Heights | tatznyc.com

TU-LU'S BAKERY

Gluten-free pastries, paninis and custom cakes. Vegan options available. A treat for those with gluten sensitivities.

338 E. 11th St. | East Village | tu-lusbakery.com

COFFEE SHOPS

BIRCH COFFEE

Organic coffee (some fair trade) and food offerings sourced from local farms.

Multiple locations | birchcoffee.com

BLUE BOTTLE COFFEE

Responsibly sourced, organic beans served no more than 48 hours
post roasting and packaged into compostable bags. Milk comes from
Battenkill Valley Creamery in Salem, NY.

Multiple locations | bluebottlecoffee.com

BROOKLYN ROASTING CO.

Organic-, fair-trade- and Rainforest Alliance-certified beans roasted in
Dumbo.

Multiple locations | brooklynroasting.com

CAFÉ PEDLAR

Stumptown Coffee roasted in Red Hook and organic milk from Ithaca,
NY, brought to you by the Frankies Spuntino (p. 110) team. Small
discount if you bring your own cup!

210 Court St. | Cobble Hill | cafepedlar.com

DAILY PRESS

Offer "buttercup" coffee made with grass fed butter and coconut oil,
along with Clementime pastries. Sources milk from Battenkill Valley
Creamery.

505 Franklin Ave. | Bedford–Stuyvesant | dailypresscoffee.com

DEVOCIÓN

Fair-trade coffee with most sourced from Columbia "red zones" with an
overall focus on hard to reach areas. Take a look at their roasting room,
visable from the street or head inside and have a seat near the veticle
garden.

69 Grand St. | Williamsburg | devocion.com

GROUNDED COFFEE
Fair-trade-certified organic teas and coffees served with organic milk (they also have other milk options) from upstate New York in a cozy environment.

28 Jane St. | West Village | groundedcoffee.com

INTELLIGENTSIA COFFEE
Direct-trade beans with a large wholesale program. The special Black Cat Project line features seasonal, micro-lot espresso.

Multiple locations | intelligentsiacoffee.com

IRVING FARM COFFEE ROASTERS
Organic coffees and transparent sourcing practices. Check out the website to learn more about its coffee farmers and estates.

Multiple locations | irvingfarm.com

JACK'S STIR BREW COFFEE
Shade-grown, fair-trade, low-acidity, organic beans served with Hudson Valley Fresh milk.

Multiple locations | jacksstirbrew.com

JOE
All of the beans are roasted in Red Hook and can be traced back to their sustainability-focused suppliers. Offers hands-on coffee classes and workshops.

Multiple locations | joenewyork.com

KAFFE 1668
Direct trade coffee with non-homogenized milk from Ronnybrook Farm in upstate New York, as well as non-dairy milk options. Also offers take-away snacks like chia pudding. Head to their other location (p.119) for a more spacious, food-filled experience.

Multiple locations | kaffe1668.com

LA COLOMBE
Focused on five principles of ethical trade: fairness, longevity of farmer relationships, opportunity, access to clean water and partnerships with estates that are certified in eco-friendly practices. Large wholesale operation.
Multiple locations | lacolombe.com

MARLTON ESPRESSO BAR
Housed in the hip Marlton Hotel, this bar brews organic coffee with house-made raw almond milk. Also provides Battenkill Valley Creamery milk for the dairy-inclined.
5 W. 8th St. | Greenwich Village | marltonhotel.com

STUMPTOWN COFFEE ROASTERS
Organic, direct-trade beans processed without chemicals. Big wholesale operation. Huge emphasis on coffee education and transparency of where it sources from—just check its website.
Multiple locations | stumptowncoffee.com

THE QUEENS KICKSHAW
Serves specialty Counter Culture coffee drinks with Battenkill Valley Creamery milk, along with kombucha, and grilled cheese made with local cheese and eggs. Gluten-free bread available. Doubles as a bar with more than 50 craft beers. Sister bar with restaurant: Wassail (p.165).
40-17 Broadway | Astoria | thequeenskickshaw.com

TOBY'S ESTATE COFFEE ROASTERS
Small-batch roasters based in Brooklyn serving single-origin coffee. Emphasizes working with farmers and cooperatives that employ sustainable practices.
Multiple locations | tobysestate.com

AMPLE HILLS CREAMERY

With its name derived from Walt Whitman's famous poem *Crossing Brooklyn Ferry*, Ample Hills excels at making ice cream using hormone-free, grass-fed cows and local ingredients.

Multiple locations | amplehills.com

BLUE MARBLE

Certified organic ice cream made with dairy from pasture-raised cows.

Multiple locations | bluemarbleicecream.com

CHLOE'S SOFT SERVE FRUIT

Soft serve made from simply fruit, water and a touch of organic cane sugar.

25 E. 17th St. | Union Square | chloesfruit.com

CULTURE

Frozen yogurt made with active, live cultures and organic milk from Hudson Valley Fresh and Organic Valley.

Multiple locations | cultureny.com

D.F. MAVENS

Dairy-free, gluten-free, cruelty-free ice cream with sugar-free options as well. The one thing it's not free of is flavor!

37 St. Marks Pl. | East Village | dfmavens.com

L'ALBERO DEI GELATI

Slow Food-approved eatery serving organic gelato made with seasonal fruit. Menu is studded with organic egg, sandwich and salad options. It also serves biodynamic wines.

341 5th Ave. | Park Slope | alberodeigelati.com

VAN LEEUWEN

All ice cream is made with antibiotic- and hormone-free dairy. The vegan ice cream is soy-free. Toby's Estate coffee is on offer.

Multiple locations | vanleeuwenicecream.com

VICTORY GARDEN

Pasture-raised goat's milk soft serve made with all local ingredients. See website for list of purveyors.

31 Carmine St. | Greenwich Village | victorygardennyc.com

JUICE BARS

3 ROOTS

Cold-pressed juices, unique smoothies and Indian-themed food options. Interesting selection of hot drinks as well.

159 Franklin St. | Greenpoint | 3rootscafe.com

CREATIVE JUICE

Organic cold-pressed juices housed in Equinox gyms.

Multiple locations | creativejuiceco.com

GINGERSNAPS ORGANIC

100% organic, cold-pressed juices and organic, vegan and raw meals to-go.

113 W. 10th St. | Greenwich Village | gingersnapsorganic.com

GRASS ROOTS JUICERY

Organic, cold-pressed juices and smoothies made with produce from local farms. Small food menu and Cafe Grumpy Coffee are also on offer.

336 Graham Ave. | Williamsburg | grassrootsjuicerybk.com

HEARTBEET JUICERY

Small window-front selling 100% organic, cold-pressed juices, house-made energy bars and a few food items. You can place orders in advance online.

85 Stanton St. | Lower East Side | heartbeetjuicery.com

JUICE GENERATION

Chain of fresh and cold-pressed juices, acai bowls, soups and raw foods. Some locations are housed in Equinox gyms.

Multiple locations | juicegeneration.com

JUICE PRESS

Huge selection of cold-pressed juices and smoothies, raw and probiotic foods. The raw oatmeal is a must-try.

Multiple locations | juicepress.com

JUICE SHOP

Milks, brews, waters, juices, tinctures, smoothies and a nice selection of food.

Muliple locations | thejuiceshopny.com

LIQUITERIA

The pioneer of cold-pressed juice in NYC. Also offering herbal supplements, healthy snacks, smoothies and grab-and-go selections.

Multiple locations | liquiteria.com

MELVIN'S JUICE BOX

Organic juices, booster shots and supplements.

Multiple locations | melvinsjuicebox.com

ORGANIC AVENUE

100% organic juices (if that wasn't obvious from the name) that are labeled according to their ingredients and super-powers like immunity, meal replacement, cleansing and daily vitamins. Also have grab-and-go options (p 139).

Multiple locations | organicaveneue.com

SUMMERS

Cold-pressed juices, sandwiches made with sustainable proteins, salads, smoothies and Devoción coffee.

155 S. 4th St. | Williamsburg | summersbrooklyn.com

TINY EMPIRE

Raw, organic juices; boosters; tinctures; shots; food to-go; and clean desserts. They also offer Blue Bottle coffee.

142 N. 6th St. | Williamsburg | tinyempirenyc.com

PROVISIONS

BROOKLYN FARE

Full grocery store with an emphasis on local products and sustainably raised, grass-fed meats. Treat yourself to a 20-course prix-fixe at Chef's Table, Brooklyn Fare's 18 seat, three Michelin-star restaurant located inside its Brooklyn location.

Multiple locations | brooklynfare.com

BKLYN LARDER

Brought to you by the Franny's (p. 111) gang, Larder stocks artisanal, locally made pantry staples, sustainably raised meats, local and raw milk cheeses and some prepared foods.

228 Flatbush Ave. | Park Slope | bklynlarder.com

BUTCHER BAR

BBQ restaurant and butcher shop serving 100% grass-fed and organic meats.

37-08 30th Ave. | Astoria | butcherbar.com

CAMPBELL CHEESE & GROCERY

Adorable shop featuring seasonal produce, artisanal goods, raw milk cheeses, kitchenware and craft beer. Carefully crafted sandwiches are available to-go.

502 Lorimer St. | Williamsburg | campbellcheese.com

DICKSON'S FARMSTAND MEATS

All meat is sourced from local farms committed to humane practices. Organic and grass-fed/finished options abound. Butcher classes on offer.

75 9th Ave. | Chelsea Market | dicksonsfarmstand.com

EL COLMADO BUTCHERY

In addition to fully prepared meals at their restaurant (p. 101), El Colmado Butchery brings in a whole, grass-fed animal each week from a local farm and allows you to purchase raw meat, game, poultry, sausage and terrine.

53 Little W. 12th St. | Meatpacking District | elcolmadonyc.com

FLEISHER'S PASTURE-RAISED MEATS

The name says it all. It uses a nose-to-tail cutting program, using all parts of the animal. It also sells soup stocks, eggs, and a small selection of artisanal condiments.

192 5th Ave. | Park Slope | fleishers.com

FORAGER'S MARKET

Wide selection of artisanal goods, pastured eggs and produce from Forager's own farm, with a juice bar and kombucha on tap, just to name a few of this market's many offerings. The Chelsea location has a kid-friendly, sit-down restaurant and biodynamic wine store attached. Plenty to forage for here.

Multiple locations | foragerscitygrocer.com

GREENE GRAPE PROVISIONS

Fish from sustainable fisheries, grass-fed meats and pantry staples all sourced as locally as possible. Some organic produce is also available.

767 Fulton St. | Fort Greene | greenegrape.com

HARLEM SHAMBLES

Non-homogenized milk, bread from Hot Bread kitchen and pastured meats. Check the website to learn more about the farms it sources from.

2141 Frederick Douglass Blvd. | Harlem | harlemshambles.com

MARLOW & DAUGHTERS

Pastured meats, house-made charcuterie and sausages and traditionally fermented, organic sourdough bread from She Wolf Bakery. Great place to pick up a housewarming gift for an uber-hip friend. Brought to you by the Diner (p. 98), Marlow & Sons (p. 128), Reynard (p. 147) and Roman's (p. 149) gang.

95 Broadway | Williamsburg | marlowanddaughters.com

THE MEAT HOOK

Large kitchenware store and whole-animal butcher shop focused on 100% grass-fed and finished meats. A paradise for any foodie, chef or chef-wanna-be. Practice your skills at one of the many cooking and butcher classes on offer.

100 Frost St. | Williamsburg | the-meathook.com

MERMAID'S GARDEN

A stunning selection of fully traceable, sustainable seafood and a selection of fish-focused prepared foods. A curated selection of pantry items round out the market's offerings.

644 Vanderbilt Ave. | Prospect Heights | mermaidsgardennyc.com

RUSS & DAUGHTERS

This "appetizing store" with a focus on sustainable, quality smoked fish, dairy products and other specialty foods also has a cafe around the corner.

179 Houston St. | Lower East Side | russanddaughters.com

SAXELBY CHEESEMONGERS

Purveyors of all-American farmstead cheeses, with a focus on the Northeast region. All cheeses come from small producers who farm sustainably with respect for their land and animals. Many raw milk cheeses available.

Multiple locations | saxelbycheese.com

VALLEY SHEPHERD CREAMERY

Hundreds of artisan food products in addition to the entire line of Valley Shepherd cheeses made from the farm's pasture-raised cows, sheeps and goats. Many raw cheese options. Looking for something to do outside of the city? Visit the farm in Long Valley, NJ—tours are available.

211 7th Ave. | Park Slope | valleyshepherd.com

WHOLE FOODS

There's plenty to choose from at this large supermarket chain that's committed to providing customers more natural and organic options as well as access to local products. Extensive produce section that demarcates local goods and a sizable bulk section. Serves as an incubator of sorts for local food start-ups.

Multiple locations | wholefoodsmarket.com

INDEX

181

185

191